Be prepared...
To learn...
To succeed...

Get **REA**dy. It all starts here. REA's preparation for the NJ ASK is **fully aligned** with the Core Curriculum Content Standards adopted by the New Jersey Department of Education.

Visit us online at
www.rea.com

READY, SET, GO!

NJ ASK
Language Arts Literacy
Grade 5

Dana Passananti
McKinley School
Westfield, New Jersey

Karen M. Magliacano
Demarest Elementary School
Bloomfield, New Jersey

Research & Education Association
Visit our website at
www.rea.com

The Performance Standards in this book were created and implemented by the New Jersey State Department of Education. For further information visit the Department of Education website at *www.state.nj.us/njded/cccs*.

Research & Education Association
61 Ethel Road West
Piscataway, New Jersey 08854
E-mail: info@rea.com

***Ready, Set, Go!*®**
New Jersey ASK
Language Arts Literacy Test
Grade 5

Printed in the United States of America

Library of Congress Control Number 2011942943

ISBN-13: 978-0-7386-1020-7
ISBN-10: 0-7386-1020-8

REA® and *Ready, Set, Go!*® are registered trademarks of Research & Education Association, Inc.

Contents

About Our Authors

Dana Passananti is a fifth grade teacher in her hometown of Westfield, N.J. She attended Saint Joseph's University, Philadelphia, Penn., where she received her degree in Elementary Education and minored in English Studies. Dana has actively volunteered as an after-school tutor at a local Philadelphia city school. In her five years of teaching, she has taken her students on overnight camping trips, space flight simulations, and walking tours of New Jersey beaches.

Dana currently lives in Westfield, N.J., with her dog, Cody. She is extremely enthusiastic about having the opportunity to help students prepare for standardized testing through the use of this book.

Karen Magliacano teaches fourth grade at Demarest Elementary School in the Bloomfield, N.J., School District. Her previous teaching experience includes pre-school, kindergarten, and second grade. As a reading specialist, she has presented numerous workshops in her district pertaining to 6 Trait writing and reading strategies. Karen is the peer coach for her school, a position that gives her the opportunity to work with new teachers, observe lessons, model new instructional strategies, provide turnkey information from professional development training, and serve as the "go-to" person in her school.

Karen received her second master's degree, in Educational Leadership, through the Fast Track Program at Montclair State University in August 2010. The degree led to a principal/supervisor certification.

About Research & Education Association

Founded in 1959, Research & Education Association (REA) is dedicated to publishing the finest and most effective educational material—including software, study guides, and test preps—for students in elementary school, middle school, high school, college, graduate school, and beyond.

Today REA's wide-ranging catalog is a leading resource for teachers, students, and professionals.

Acknowledgments

We would like to thank REA's Larry B. Kling, Vice President, Editorial, for supervising development; Pam Weston, Publisher, for setting the quality standards for production integrity and managing the publication to completion; Alice Leonard, Senior Editor, for production management and editorial integrity; and Fred N. Grayson of American BookWorks Corporation for overseeing manuscript development and typesetting and preflight editorial review. Our cover was designed by Christine Saul, Senior Graphic Designer.

Chapter 1
Succeeding on the NJ ASK Grade 5
Language Arts Literacy Test

This book holds the keys to your success on the NJ ASK Grade 5 Language Arts Literacy Test. Here you'll find everything you need to succeed, including:

- Focused subject review
- Many examples to reinforce your mastery in each content area
- Two full-length practice tests in the same format as the actual test

We encourage you to work through the book from front to back. Some areas may be newer to you than others. Still, by the end of each section, you will have a good idea about where you need to put in more time and what you are comfortable with for test day.

USING THIS BOOK

This book focuses on reading and writing instruction and practice. There are **two lesson sections:**

Chapter 2: You will find assorted reading skills and passages within this chapter. Each skill has **two** practice activities. One activity will focus on open-ended or

1

paragraph responses. The other activity will focus on multiple-choice, matching, or fill-in-the-blank type answers.

Chapter 3: You will find various writing prompts and tips within the writing portion of this section. The chapter starts off by explaining the two types of writing you will need to respond to in a timely fashion. Next, a **prewriting** section is introduced with an opportunity to practice organizing your thoughts and ideas. Here we give you a brief outline about how you can set up your writing. This chapter concludes with a brief instruction on how to revise and edit your writing piece.

Finally, this book concludes with **two full-length practice tests** mirrored from NJ ASK Grade 5 Language Arts Literacy tests from previous years. Following each test, we provide you with answers and complete explanations.

WHAT'S ON THE TEST

The New Jersey Department of Education sets the following goals for the NJ ASK testing program:

- To measure and promote student achievement of challenging state curriculum standards

- To provide accurate and meaningful information about student performance

- To meet state and federal accountability requirements

The format of the test for Grade 5 includes two days of Language Arts Literacy assessment. There are **three** reading passages at grade level for fifth grade students to read, analyze, and answer questions based on the reading. Sometimes you will need to draw on personal experiences. The reading passages you will encounter are both fiction and nonfiction, ranging from literary and informational to everyday text. Expect a wide range of genres and sources for each selection.

The writing portion of the test will focus on two types of writing: expository and speculative. Writing tasks require students to respond in a variety of modes and forms for a variety of purposes. Some may present a brief scenario for an imaginative story, while others may ask students to reflect on a personal memory, time, and place. Students will be given 30 minutes to respond to the writing task. Further explanation of writing tasks can be found in Chapter 3.

All practice test questions are based on NJ ASK Grade 5 Language Arts Literacy Content Clusters and Skills, as detailed below:

New Jersey Core Curriculum Content Standards – Grade 5 Literacy	Related Content Found in Practice Test 1	Related Content Found in Practice Test 2
STANDARD 3.1 (Reading) All students will understand and apply the knowledge of sounds, letters, and words in written English to become independent and fluent readers, and will read a variety of materials and texts with fluency and comprehension.		
3.1.5. A. Concepts About Print / Text		
2. Survey and explain text features that contribute to comprehension (e.g., headings, introductory and concluding paragraphs).	Day 1 Section 1 and 3 Day 2 Section 1	Day 1 and Day 2 Sections 1 and 3
3.1.5. C. Decoding and Word Recognition		
2. Use context clues or knowledge of phonics, syllabication, prefixes, and suffixes to decode new words.	Day 1 Section 1 #2 Day 1, Section 3 # 4 ,6 and 7	Day 1, Section 1, #2, Section 3, # 8 Day 2, Section 1, #4
3. Interpret new words correctly in context.	Day 1 Section 1#10 Day 1 Section 3 #4, 6, and 7	Day 1, Section 1, #2, Section 3, #8 Day 2, Section 1, #4
3.1.5. D. Fluency		
1. Adjust reading speed appropriately for different purposes and audiences.	Day 1 Section 1 and 3 Day 2 Section 1	Day 1, Sections 1 and 3 Day 2, Section 1
4. Read silently for the purpose of increasing speed, accuracy, and reading fluency.	Day 1 Section 1 and 3 Day 2 Section 1	Day 1, Sections 1 and 3 Day 2, Section 1

3.1.5. E. Reading Strategies (before, during, and after reading)		Practice Test 2
1. Activate prior knowledge and anticipate what will be read or heard.	Day 1 Section 1 and 3 Day 2 Section 1	Day 1 Sections 1 and 3 Day 2 Section 1
2. Vary reading strategies according to their purpose for reading and the nature of the text.	Day 1 Section 1 and 3 Day 2 Section 1	Day 1 Sections 1 and 3 Day 2 Section 1
3. Reread to make sense of difficult paragraphs or sections of text.	Day 1 Section 1 and 3 Day 2 Section 1	Day 1, Sections 1 and 3 Day 2 Section 1
4. Make revisions to text predictions during and after reading.	Day 1 Section 1 and 3 Day 2 Section 1	Day 1 Sections 1 and 3 Day 2, Section 1
3.1.5. F. Vocabulary and Concept Development		
1. Infer word meanings from learned roots, prefixes, and suffixes.	Day 1 Section 1 and 3 Day 2 Section 1 Day 1 Section 3 #6 and 7	Day 1, Section 1, #2, Section 3, #8 Day 2, Section 2, #1, 4
2. Infer specific word meanings in the context of reading passages.	Day 1 Section 1 #10 Day 1 Section 3 #4, 6, and 7 Day 2 Section 1 #5 and 9	Day 1, Section 1 #2, Section 3, #8
3.1.5. G. Comprehension Skills and Response to Text		
1. Identify author's purpose, views, and beliefs.	Day 1 Section 1 #6 Day 1 Section 3 #5 Day 2 Section 1 #1, 2, 5, 6, and 9	Day 1, Section 1, #1, Section 3, #9 Day 2, Section 1 #9
2. Identify genre by their distinctive elements (e.g., tall tale-exaggeration).	Day 1 Section 1 and 3 Day 2 Section 1	Day 1 and Day 2 Sections 1 and 3

4. Anticipate and construct meaning from text by making conscious connections to self, an author, and others.	Day 1. Section 1 #1-4, 8, 9, and 11 Day 1 Section 3 #8 and 11 Day 2 Section 1 #7, 8, and 11	Day 1 and Day 2 Sections 1 and 3
7. Understand that theme refers to the central idea or meaning of a selection and recognize themes, whether implied or stated directly.	Day 1 Section 1 # 7 and 11 Day 1 Section 3 #1, 9, and 11 Day 2 Section 1 #8 and 11	Day 1 and Day 2 Sections 1 and 3
8. Distinguish between major and minor details.	Day 1 Section 3 #1, 2, and 11 Day 2 Section 1 #2 and 8	Day 1, Section 1, #5, Section 3, #1, 5
9. Make inferences using textual information and provide supporting evidence.	Day 1 Section 1 #1, 2, 4, 8, and 9 Day 1 Section 3 #8, 9 Dat 2 Section 1 #3, 4, 5, and 9	Day 1, Section 1, #3, 10, Section 3, #5, 7 Day 2, Section 1, #7
11. Identify and analyze text types, formats, and elements in nonfiction.	Day 1 Section 1 and 3 Day 2 Section 1	Day 1 and Day 2 Sections 1 and 3
12. Recognize literary elements in stories, including setting, characters, plot, and mood.	Day 1 Section 1 and 3 Day 2 Section 1	Day 1 and Day 2 Sections 1 and 3
13. Recognize figurative language in text (e.g., simile, metaphor, personification, alliteration).	Day 1 Section 1 #5 and 6 Day 2 Section 1 #10	Day 2, Section 1, #2
3.1.5. H. Inquiry and Research		
5. Draw conclusions from information gathered from multiple sources.	Day 1 Section 1 and 3 Day 2 Section 1	Day 1 and Day 2 Sections 1 and 3

New Jersey Core Curriculum Content Standards – Grade 5 Literacy	Related Content	Related Content
STANDARD 3.2 (writing) all students will write in clear, concise, organized language that varies in content and form for different audiences and purposes.		
3.2.5. A. Writing as a Process (Prewriting, drafting, revising, editing, post-writing)		
1. Write stories with multiple paragraphs that develop a situation or plot, describe the setting, and include an ending.	Day 1 Section 2	Day 1, Section 2
2. Write informational compositions with multiple paragraphs that present important ideas, provide details, and offer a concluding paragraph.	Day 2 Section 2	Day 1, Section 2
3. Generate possible ideas for writing through listening, talking, recalling experiences, hearing stories, reading, discussing models of writing, asking questions, and brainstorming.	Day 1 Section 2 Day 2 Section 2	Day 1 Section 1, #11, Section 2, Section 3, #10 Day 2, Section 1, #10
5. Use strategies such as graphic organizers and outlines to elaborate and organize ideas for writing.	Day 1 Section 2 Day 2 Section 2	Day 1 Section 2 Day 2 Section 2
6. Draft writing in a selected genre with supporting structure according to the intended message, audience, and purpose for writing	Day 1 Section 2 Day 2 Section 2	Day 1 Section 2 Day 2 Section 2
7. Make decisions about the use of precise language, including adjectives, adverbs, verbs, and specific details, and justify the choices made.	Day 1 Section 1 #11 Day 1 Section 2 Day 1 Section 3 #11 Day 2 Section 1 #11 Day 2 Section 2	Day 1 Section 1, #11, Section 3, #10 Day 2 Section 1, #10
8. Revise drafts by rereading for meaning, narrowing focus, elaborating and deleting, as well as reworking organization, openings, closings, word choice, and consistency of voice.	Day 1 Section 1 #11 Day 1 Section 2 Day 1 Section 3 #11 Day 2 Section 1 #11 Day 2 Section 2	Day 1 Section 1, #11, Section 3, #10 Day 2 Section 1, #10, Section 2

10. Review and edit work for spelling, usage, clarity, organization, and fluency.	Day 1 Section 1 #11 Day 1 Section 2 Day 1 Section 3 #11 Day 2 Section 1 #11 Day 2 Section 2	Day 1 Section 1, #11, Section 2, Section 3, #10. Day 2, Section 1 Section 2, #10

3.2.5. B. Writing as a Product (resulting in a formal product or publication)	Related Content	Related Content
1. Expand knowledge of characteristics and structures of selected genres.	Day 1 Section 3 Day 2 Section 1	Day 1 Section 1 and 3
2. Write a range of grade appropriate essays across curricula (e.g., persuasive, personal, descriptive, issue-based)	Day 1 Section 2 Day 2 Section 2	Day 1 Section 2 Day 2 Section 2
3. Write grade appropriate, multi-paragraph, expository pieces across curricula (e.g., problem/solution, cause/effect, hypothesis/results, feature articles, critique, research reports).	Day 1 Section 1 #11 Day 2 Section 2	Day 1 Section 1, #11 Section 2, Section 3, #10 Day 2 Section 1, #10, Section 2
4. Write various types of prose, such as short stories, biography, autobiography, or memoir, that contain narrative elements.	Day 1 Section 2 Day 2 Section 2	Day 1 Section 1, #11 Section 2, Section 3, #10 Day 2 Section 1, #10, Section 2
5. Support main idea, topic, or theme with facts, examples, or explanations, including information from multiple sources.	Day 1 Section 1#11 Day 1 Section 2 Day 1Section 3#11 Day 2 Section 1#11 Day 2 Section 2	Day 1 Section 1, #11 Section 2, Section 3, #10 Day 2 Section 1, #10, Section 2
6. Sharpen focus and improve coherence by considering the relevancy of included details and adding, deleting, and rearranging appropriately.	Day 1 Section #11 Day 1 Section 2 Day 1 Section 3#11 Day 2 Section 1#11 Day 2 Section 2	Day 1 Section 1, #11 Section 2, Section 3, #10 Day 2 Section 1, #10, Section 2

7. Write sentences of varying length and complexity, using specific nouns, verbs, and descriptive words.	Day 1 Section 1#11 Day 1 Section 2 Day 1 Section 3#11 Day 2 Section 1#11 Day 2 Section 2	Day 1 Section 1, #11 Section 2, Section 3, #10 Day 2 Section 1, #10, Section 2
9. Provide logical sequence throughout multi-paragraph works by refining organizational structure and developing transitions between ideas.	Day 1 Section 1#11 Day 1 Section 2 Day 1 Section 3#11 Day 2 Section 1#11 Day 2 Section 2	Day 1 Section 1, #11 Section 2, Section 3, #10 Day 2 Section 1, #10, Section 2
10. Engage the reader from beginning to end with an interesting opening, logical sequence, and satisfying conclusion.	Day 1 Section 1#11 Day 1 Section 2 Day 1 Section 3#11 Day 2 Section 1#11 Day 2 Section 2	Day 1 Section 1, #11 Section 2, Section 3, #10 Day 2 Section 1, #10, Section 2

3.2.5. C. Mechanics, Spelling, and Handwriting

1. Use Standard English conventions in all writing, such as sentence structure, grammar and usage, punctuation, capitalization, spelling, and handwriting.	Day 1 Section 1#11 Day 1 Section 2 Day 1 Section 3#11 Day 2 Section 1#11 Day 2 Section 2	Day 1 Section 1, #11, Section 2, Section 3, #10 Day 2 Section 1, #10, Section 2
2. Use increasingly complex sentence structure and syntax to express ideas.	Day 1 Section 1#11 Day 1 Section 2 Day 1 Section 3#11 Day 2 Section 1#11 Day 2 Section 2	Day 1 Section 1, #11, Section 2, Section 3, #10 Day 2 Section 1, #10, Section 2
3. Use knowledge of English grammar and usage to express ideas effectively.	Day 1 Section 1#11 Day 1 Section 2 Day 1 Section 3#11 Day 2 Section 1#11 Day 2 Section 2	Day 1 Section 1, #11, Section 2, Section 3, #10 Day 2 Section 1, #10, Section 2
4. Use correct capitalization and punctuation, including commas and colons, throughout writing.	Day 1 Section 1#11 Day 1 Section 2 Day 1 Section 3#11 Day 2 Section 1#11 Day 2 Section 2	Day 1 Section 1, #11, Section 2, Section 3, #10 Day 2 Section 1, #10, Section 2

5. Use quotation marks and related punctuation correctly in passages of dialogue.	Day 1 Section 1#11 Day 1 Section 2 Day 1 Section 3#11 Day 2 Section 1#11 Day 2 Section 2	Day 1 Section 1, #11, Section 2, Section 3, #10 Day 2 Section 1, #10, Section 2
6. Use knowledge of roots, prefixes, suffixes, and English spelling patterns to spell words correctly in writing.	Day 1 Section 1#11 Day 1 Section 2 Day 1 Section 3#11 Day 2 Section 1#11 Day 2 Section 2	Day 1 Section 1, #11, Section 2, Section 3, #10 Day 2 Section 1, #10, Section 2
8. Edit writing for correct grammar usage, capitalization, punctuation, and spelling.	Day 1 Section 1#11 Day 1 Section 2 Day 1 Section 3#11 Day 2 Section 1#11 Day 2 Section 2	Day 1 Section 1, #11, Section 2, Section 3, #10 Day 2 Section 1, #10, Section 2
3.2.5. D. Writing Forms, Audiences, and Purposes (exploring a variety of forms)		
1. Write for different purposes (e.g., to express ideas, inform, entertain, respond to literature, persuade, question, reflect, clarify, share) and a variety of audiences (e.g., self, peers, community).	Day 1 Section 1#11 Day 1 Section 2 Day 1 Section 3#11 Day 2 Section 1#11 Day 2 Section 2	Day 1 Section 1, #11, Section 2, Section 3, #10 Day 2 Section 1, #10, Section 2
2. Gather, select, and organize information appropriate to a topic, task, and audience.	Day 1 Section 1#11 Day 1 Section 2 Day 1 Section 3#11 Day 2 Section 1#11 Day 2 Section 2	Day 1 Section 1, #11, Section 2, Section 3, #10 Day 2 Section 1, #10, Section 2
3. Develop and use knowledge of a variety of genres, including expository, narrative, persuasive, poetry, critiques, and everyday/workplace writing.	Day 1 Section 1#11 Day 1 Section 2 Day 1 Section 3#11 Day 2 Section 1#11 Day 2 Section 2	Day 1 Section 1, #11, Section 2, Section 3, #10 Day 2 Section 1, #10, Section 2
4. Organize a response that develops insight into literature by exploring personal reactions, connecting to personal experiences, and referring to the text through sustained use of examples.	Day 1 Section 1#11 Day 1 Section 2 Day 1 Section 3#11 Day 2 Section 1#11 Day 2 Section 2	Day 1 Section 1, #11, Section 2, Section 3, #10 Day 2 Section 1, #10, Section 2

5. Use transitions between and within paragraphs.	Day 1 Section 1#11 Day 1 Section 2 Day 1 Section 3#11 Day 2 Section 1#11 Day 2 Section 2	Day 1 Section 1, #11, Section 2, Section 3, #10 Day 2 Section 1, #10, Section 2
6. Organize paragraphs using topic sentences.	Day 1 Section 1#11 Day 1 Section 2 Day 1 Section 3#11 Day 2 Section 1#11 Day 2 Section 2	Day 1 Section 1, #11, Section 2, Section 3, #10 Day 2 Section 1, #10, Section 2
7. Write narratives, establishing a plot or conflict, setting, characters, point of view, and resolution.	Day 1 Section 1#11 Day 1 Section 2 Day 1 Section 3#11 Day 2 Section 1#11 Day 2 Section 2	Day 1 Section 1, #11, Section 2, Section 3, #10 Day 2 Section 1, #10, Section 2
8. Use narrative techniques (e.g., dialogue, specific actions of characters, sensory description, and expression of thoughts and feelings of characters).	Day 1 Section 1#11 Day 1 Section 2 Day 1 Section 3#11 Day 2 Section 1#11 Day 2 Section 2	Day 1 Section 1, #11, Section 2, Section 3, #10 Day 2 Section 1, #10, Section 2
12. Use a variety of strategies to organize writing, including sequence, chronology, cause/ effect, problem/solution, and order of importance.	Day 1 Section 1#11 Day 1 Section 2 Day 1 Section 3#11 Day 2 Section 1#11 Day 2 Section 2	Day 1 Section 1, #11, Section 2, Section 3, #10 Day 2 Section 1, #10, Section 2
13. Demonstrate higher-order thinking skills and writing clarity when answering open-ended and essay questions in content areas or as responses to literature.	Day 1 Section 1#11 Day 1 Section 2 Day 1 Section 3#11 Day 2 Section 1#11 Day 2 Section 2	Day 1 Section 1, #11, Section 2, Section 3, #10 Day 2 Section 1, #10, Section 2
15. Demonstrate the development of a personal style and voice in writing.	Day 1 Section 1#11 Day 1 Section 2 Day 1 Section 3#11 Day 2 Section 1#11 Day 2 Section 2	Day 1 Section 1, #11, Section 2, Section 3, #10 Day 2 Section 1, #10, Section 2

PREPARING FOR THE TEST

Tips for Teachers

As with most standardized testing, students may feel an overwhelming sense of anxiety. As teachers, we must remind students that there is nothing to be nervous about. Using this book will guide you in working on and monitoring the progress of each child. Preparing students with time management skills and reviewing the work they've completed will give them the confidence they need to succeed on the NJ ASK.

Here are a few reminders for your students to help make the testing experience easier.

1. Get a full night's sleep before testing.

2. Eat a good breakfast so he/she has plenty of energy.

3. Dress comfortably.

4. Get to school on time.

Tips for Parents

Students work hard all year long on being organized, using their time wisely and being responsible for their school work. Reminding them to use those skills on the test will reinforce the notion that hard work pays off. Prior to the test, stay in close contact with your child's teacher so that you know what skills need more reinforcement. Provide a nurturing learning environment for homework and projects and commend your child on his/her hard work and dedication.

Here are a few important reminders to give your child for test day.

1. Pay close attention to the directions given by your teacher. If you don't understand, it is important to ask for help.

2. Answer the questions that are easy first, then go back to work on the more difficult questions.

3. Work at a steady pace – don't rush.

4. Write answers neatly.

5. If you have extra time, go back and check your work.

6. Only change an answer if you are sure it is wrong.

Thank you for helping to provide your child with a successful NJ ASK experience!

Chapter 2
Reading Comprehension

OVERVIEW

The Language Arts Literacy component of the NJ ASK 5 requires students to work, analyze, critique, and interpret a variety of texts, illustrations, and activities. The Language Arts Literacy component is given over two days. During those two days your test will consist of two sections that will require reading a passage, answering multiple-choice questions, and preparing a response to an open-ended question or prompt.

Reading Comprehension requires you to hold ideas and think critically about what you are reading. You should try to connect the ideas in order to gain a better understanding of the **main idea** surrounding each passage. Constant questioning before, during, and after reading provides you with the framework and motivation to retain the information you are reviewing. If you pay close attention to the supporting details and cues, you can gain insight into the author's mind.

Reading Comprehension Tips

It does not matter what the question asks, if you remember to apply certain tips.

Read the following tips before starting the exercises in this chapter:

 Take Your Time: At the beginning of each test, your teacher will tell you how long you will have to complete each section. As you practice using this book, have someone time you so that you are aware of how much longer you have. Do not rush through any section, but make sure you have enough time to check your work.

 **<u>Use the Text as a Resource</u>**: Think about what you know before you begin reading. This way, you may activate some prior knowledge! If you read a detail or word you think might be important, underline or make notes in the margins or on the side. You'll be more focused on the end result and you will pick up on important details as you read. Although nothing in your test booklet will be scored, it's a great resource to use if you begin to run out of time. You'll have some notes that you could quickly skim to find the answers to the questions.

 **<u>Do Your Best:</u>** Even when you feel prepared, there may be some things you come across during the reading section about which you are unsure of. Do not let big words, places, and names trip you up. Skip over them for the time being and only come back to them if you need to answer a question that refers to that subject. If you understand what you're reading, you are on the right track!

 **<u>Check Your Work</u>**: If you have time, go back and check what you have just worked on. Sometimes, you need "fresh eyes" to catch spelling, grammar, and silly mistakes. For open-ended responses, go back to see if you can add more details or perhaps a "bigger" vocabulary word.

OPEN-ENDED RESPONSES

The ability to answer open-ended responses on the NJ ASK5 is very important. At the end of each reading passage, you will need to respond, in writing, by working or analyzing a question about the text. An open-ended question is designed to encourage a meaningful response. It sometimes asks you to reflect or add a personal feeling. **Why, how, explain the way**, or **summarize** are all key words to look for. In an open-ended response, you should provide as much detail as possible and make sure you hit on all the questions asked. Your answer should be organized and about a paragraph in length.

Throughout this Reading chapter, you will be confronted with open-ended responses. Try your hardest to draw on the text and provide details explaining why and how. Be sure to add your personal feeling when prompted to do so.

LITERARY ELEMENTS

Literary elements help make fiction and non-fiction passages appealing, interesting, and memorable to the reader. Writers use these devices and techniques to communicate their ideas. Often, the author uses figurative language or imagery to describe a situation or character without actually *telling* the reader what to think. This allows readers to create their own mental picture. Good writers "show" their story without telling.

Become acquainted with the terms that you may come across in the questions or the reading passages. The more you review these literary elements now, the more prepared you will be on test day!

Whenever you describe something by comparing it with something else, you are using **figurative language.**

Simile: Compares two things. One of the things is compared to something unlike itself. Example: "My day was as long as a football field."

Metaphor: Compares two unlike things and is very straightforward and does not use "like" or "as."
Example: "My house is an old dinosaur."

Personification: Gives something human qualities or characteristics.
Example: "The trees sang a sweet song."

Onomatopoeia: Uses a word to describe the sound it makes.
Example: "CRASH!"

Plot: The series of events in a story.

Characterization: Describes qualities and actions an individual displays during the story.

Point of View: The perspective from which the story is told. It could be told by a narrator or someone who is watching the action.

Imagery: Vivid language that helps the reader paint a mental picture of what's going on in the story.

Problem: Something that goes wrong or in a different direction throughout the course of the story.

Solution: The way in which the problem is fixed by someone in the story.

Exercise 1: Literary Elements

Directions: Read the passage below and complete the activities that follow. Be sure to answer all parts of the question and support with evidence from the text, if necessary.

OPENING DAY DELIGHT

"Going...... Going......GONE!" I shouted as I cracked my wooden baseball bat against Jimmy's brand new, perfectly red-stitched Rawlings baseball. We were getting ready to attend Opening Day at Champions Stadium. We could hardly wait and slept like you do the night before the first day of school.

Opening Day provides memorable experiences for baseball lovers all around the world. Fans from all over gather at their favorite stadiums, adorned in their favorite team's gear, and expect a game full of joy and delight. Jimmy and I were as ready as ever. We carefully helped my mom pack the car and we were on our way.

"Hey, Rick!" Jimmy shouted from the backseat. "Where exactly are our seats?"

"First base side, right behind my favorite player, Bradley Peterson!" exclaimed Rick.

When we finally arrived, it was as if the Stadium walls were speaking to me. They were inviting me in, persuading me to buy a new jersey, and tempting me with the appetizing smells from the food vendors. This was Jimmy's first time at Champions Stadium. He was as excited as a kid in a candy story. Jimmy didn't know where to look first! The green grass shimmered with dew, and the Champions' Playoff flags waved in the near distance. The smell of freshly waxed baseball bats and buttered popcorn filled the air.

"Row C, Seat 18!" I screamed in the direction of my mom and Jimmy. I couldn't tell if I was walking excessively fast or if they were just walking at a snail's pace. "Eeeeeeeeeeek!" My sneakers screamed as I came to a screeching halt. There, in my peripheral vision, was Bradley Peterson. He caught my eye as the locker room door was rapidly closing. He was suiting up for today's game. His baseball socks were pulled over his gray trimmed pants and his cap was full-brimmed and rested nicely upon his head. Before I could call to Mom and Jimmy, the door was shut, and I knew it was game time.

"HURRY UP!" I belted out. We rushed to our seats in order to make the last of the opposing team's batting practice and to hear the starting line-up. I could hardly contain my excitement. I couldn't believe that I, Rick Patessa, 13 years old, was about to watch my favorite team play on their biggest day of the season. Normally, I would be excited, but today's emotions were heightened. I had my best friend with me, my mom who graciously bought and paid for the tickets, and my dad's old, worn in Mizuno baseball glove. I was determined to catch a foul ball, or at the very least, come close to one. I know the odds of actually catching one are slim to none, but a kid can dream!

"And now for the Crusaders' Starting Line-Up!" wailed the announcer. He introduced each player, their number, and most importantly, their position. I was overjoyed!

"Uh, Rick? Where is Bradley Peterson?" "He wasn't called to play First Base." Jimmy wondered.

"What? How did I miss that? I must have been so excited about our seats," Rick gestured.

Instantaneously, my mood changed from a bright neon yellow to a dark and solemn blue. The best part of today's game was our seats being so close to my favorite player. I didn't want Jimmy to know how upset I was so I tried to hide my feelings. I adjusted my glove and my mood and tried to enjoy the momentous occasion that was Opening Day.

"May I have everyone's attention, please?" roared the announcer. "We have a special, Opening Day giveaway before the Crusaders take the field and throw out the first pitch!"

"Wooooooo!" I cheered. Maybe today would be better after all. I had a million thoughts running through my head; "Maybe they'll call someone to be their new bat boy!" I hoped.

"Or maybe they're giving away season tickets!" exclaimed Jimmy.

"Now it's time to call our winner!" broadcasted the announcer. His voice was as sharp as a blade. When he spoke, everyone listened. "If you're a winner, you'll have an orange Crusaders' sticker stuck to the bottom of your stadium seat," he declared.

"Crrriiiickkkkk," went the sound of my seat. I pulled the top up slowly and bent down to check and see if I was the winner. I lay my baseball mitt down and slid under the seat to get a closer look.

"Holy Cannoli, Mom! It's me! I'm the winner!" I cried out. "I can't believe this!"

"Wow, Rick. You are one lucky 13-year-old. I wonder what prize you've won!" congratulated Jimmy.

"Rick Patessa, please make your way to Gate F23. Please make your way to Gate F23 to receive your prize," confirmed the announcer.

I hurried my way all the way to gate F23, and there, standing underneath the purple canopy, was Bradley Peterson. He had a crisp white envelope in his hand and a smile on his face.

"Rick?" Bradley questioned.

"Yess-uh- that's me!" I stuttered. "You are my favorite player, Bradley, and I never win anything. Thanks for making this day so special."

"Work hard, play hard, right Rick? That's how it goes. Here in this envelope are four tickets to next week's home game against the Pirates. I hope you can make it," Peterson said. "Oh, and one more thing, wear this when you throw out the first pitch next week. Don't let me down, you'll be wearing my jersey!" whispered Peterson.

By the time I caught my breath to say "thank you" or "I'll be practicing," he was gone. The next thing I knew, I heard the roar of the crowd and the crunchy sounds of the keyboard playing the National Anthem. I returned to my seat to give the details about my winnings to Jimmy and my mom. Jimmy was a ghost. His face went white and he couldn't speak. My mom was a cheerleader; hugging and kissing me and screaming "Ooh, Ricky!"

It was the best day ever. I was as excited as a baseball player on opening day, except this time, I was a part of it all. PLAY BALL!

1. From whose point of view is the story told? Explain your reasoning.

_____

_____

_____

_____

_____

_____

2. Where does the story take place? Use examples of the text to support your answer.

_____

_____

_____

_____

_____

_____

3. In a well-organized paragraph, summarize the plot of this passage.

_____

_____

_____

_____

_____

_____

_____

_____

_____

4. In the second to last paragraph, the main character says, "My mom was a cheerleader." What was he comparing?

_____

_____

_____

_____

_____

_____

_____

5. Explain what the onomatopoeia "Crrriiiickkkkk" was used for. What did the author want the reader to feel?

_____

_____

_____

_____

_____

_____

_____

Exercise 1 Answers:

1. "Opening Day Delight" was told from the point of view of Rick Patessa, the main character. In paragraph 7, it reads, "I couldn't believe that I, Rick Patessa, 13 years old, was about to watch my favorite team play on their biggest game of the season."

2. "Row C, Seat 18!" *Opening Day Delight* takes place in Champions Stadium. In paragraph 5, the author writes, "This was Jimmy's first time at Champions Stadium."

3. The main plot of this story is about Rick Patessa and his friend Jimmy attending Opening Day for their favorite baseball team at Champions Stadium. Rick couldn't wait to see his favorite player, Bradley Peterson. After the line-up was announced and a giveaway was promised, Rick won the giveaway and a chance to throw out the first pitch at an upcoming home game. He was also able to meet his favorite player and wear his new jersey.

4. The main character says "My mom was a cheerleader" to compare his mom's reaction to his winning free tickets and the chance to throw out the first pitch. It showed that his mom was excited and cheering to congratulate him on his winnings.

5. "Crrriiiickkkkk, went the sound of my seat." The author uses example of this onomatopoeia to create suspense for the reader as Rick looked under his seat for the Crusaders' sticker that would indicate he had won the giveaway.

Exercise 2: Literary Elements

Directions: Read the passage below and complete the activities that follow. Be sure to read all parts of the question before deciding on a final answer.

PICTURE PERFECT

As upsetting as it may be to your parents, there is no escaping fighting with your brothers or sisters. Even though it's routine and normal, it doesn't make it any less frustrating!

Every day, my sister Ana and I fight over who gets to use the bathroom first. I guess it wouldn't be as bad if Ana didn't take over an hour when she was in there. I usually just run in the shower, run out, brush my teeth, and I'm on my way. Ana, on the other hand, takes forever to get ready.

"Megan! You're using up all the hot water, and today is picture day! My hair needs to look stylish and popular," Ana trailed off.

"Popular? How does your hairstyle make you popular?" I asked, confused. "And, I've only been in here five minutes, hold your horses!"

I didn't even realize it was picture day. I was about as clueless as a baby. Being twins in middle school is serious stuff. My sister, Ana, was a bit more alert when it came to social events. I, on the other hand, was more worried about my grades and studying for big tests. Even though we are twins, we couldn't be more different.

After the bathroom debacle, we made our way to school. I made sure I had everything I needed for the day before we left. Ana, still rushing around after taking 30 minutes to style her "popular" hairstyle just grabbed her backpack and left. Her backpack practically cried every time she picked it up. It has so much stuff in there and it was usually pretty stinky and smelly, let alone dirty.

When we walked into our homeroom, our teacher reminded us to take out our purple picture day forms. For a second, I was in sheer panic. "Had I forgotten to pack the form?" I thought to myself. Then again, who was I kidding? Mom filled out the form a week in advance, just as I requested. Ana, on the other hand, looked like she just stepped off a rollercoaster. Her face was distorted and she looked like she was going to be sick. So much for that popular hairstyle.

"Pssst! Meg! I don't have my form. Did Mom pack it with yours by accident?" she asked, nervously.

"Nope, sorry Ana, it's not in here," I replied. I felt pretty bad since she was so eager to have her picture taken. I did my very best to try and cheer her up, but nothing was working. At this point, she began to cry and her eyes were red and puffy like a rash.

"Let's go, boys and girls, we are headed to the gym!" our teacher shouted. Ana didn't have much time to come up with a solution. She skulked all the way the gym. I felt awful, so I followed behind.

As we lined up in alphabetical order, Ana looked around and realized that everyone had a purple form in their hands. She felt like a kid being left out on the playground.

"How am I going to have my picture taken if I don't have the form, Meg?" asked Ana. "You're smart, come up with something!" she pleaded.

I don't know what came over me, but I took out my favorite blue gel pen, crossed out my name and wrote in Ana's.

"I'll take mine during picture re-takes. You worked really hard on your hairstyle this morning and it looks great," I said, paying her an overdue compliment.

1. The simile "She felt like a kid being left out on the playground" shows that
   A. Ana was happy that she was outside.
   B. Ana thought she was the only one in school who forgot the form.
   C. Ana was disappointed that her sister didn't remind her.
   D. Ana wanted to relieve her stress by playing on the playground.

2. The problem in this story was that
   A. Ana and Meg weren't great friends.
   B. Ana and Meg are very similar since they're twins.
   C. Ana forgot her picture form.
   D. Meg was extremely organized.

3. From whose point of view is the story told?
   A. Ana's
   B. Meg's
   C. The photographer's
   D. It was told by a narrator who was observing the actions of both Ana and Meg.

4. The author gives a detailed description of Meg and Ana's relationship to illustrate that Meg and Ana

    A. are twins but have very different personalities.

    B. both hang out with the same people.

    C. can't work together.

    D. always agree with each other.

5. The sentence, "Her backpack practically cried every time she picked it up," is an example of what literary element?

    A. imagery

    B. simile

    C. metaphor

    D. personification

6. Describe what Meg's solution to Ana's problem demonstrates about Meg's character.

_____

_____

_____

_____

_____

_____

_____

_____

_____

_____

Exercise 2 Answers:

1. **B**

   The simile "She felt like a kid being left out on the playground" shows a comparison between being left out and Ana forgetting her form.

2. **C**

   The problem was not that she and her sister weren't great friends. Ana and Meg are similar because they are twins, but that is not the problem in the story. Letter D isn't relevant to the question.

3. **B**

   The story is told from Meg's point of view. In the passage, Meg says, "My sister, Ana, was a bit more alert when it came to social events. I, on the other hand, was more worried about my grades and studying for big tests."

4. **A**

   The author is providing details about their relationship to hint to us that although they are twins there are several qualities in which they differ. Choices B, C, and D give examples that aren't made clear to the reader in the passage.

5. **D**

   Personification is a literary element that gives human qualities to things that do not normally possess them. The sentence, "Her backpack practically cried every time she picked it up," shows that her backpack was quite unhappy because it was carrying several items.

6. **Possible answer:** "I don't know what came over me, but I took out my favorite blue gel pen, crossed out my name, and wrote in Ana's name." When Meg gave her slip to Ana, it showed that Meg may fight with her sister, but she also loves, cares, and respects her. Meg shows good character by understanding Ana's problem and coming up with a solution that is fair for both of them. Although Meg will have her picture taken later, she knew that her sister was looking forward to it and spent much time getting ready. In the end, Meg did the right thing and showed admirable character.

MAKING INFERENCES

Making inferences is an essential part of reading comprehension. As you are reading, you are constantly looking for clues or subtle hints that lead you to what is going to happen next. Essentially, when you are inferring, you are looking for things that aren't there, but are using hints from the text, and any background knowledge you have, to make an informed decision. When you are actively reading, you are making inferences and piecing together the clues the author gives you. Making predictions and personal connections will also help you to "think outside the box" and read between the lines. Since the author doesn't give you the answer, it is up to you to figure out the best answer with the information you are given.

When you are learning to make inferences, you should ask yourself questions as you read. Here are a few tips you can use when you start practicing this skill:

- What do I already know about this topic?

- What was the main idea about the passage?

- What clues did the author provide to help me reach a conclusion?

- What did the author really mean when he/she said….?

- How are the details connected to the main idea of the story?

Exercise 3: Making Inferences

Directions: Read the passage below and complete the activities that follow. Be sure to read all parts of the question before deciding on a final answer.

OVERNIGHT CAMPING TRIP

 Kayla and Pamela were two of the best Junior Girl scouts in Troop 730. Every year they volunteered to help out at bake sales and nursing homes. They helped organize a craft fair last winter, and always sell more than their fair share of Girl Scout cookies each spring. When the final count for the winners of the Girl Scout cookie challenge was about to be announced, Kayla and Pamela hoped and wished they would be the recipients of the overnight camping trip for their troop.

As Thursday night approached, the girls gathered at Mrs. Sadrock's house to engage in their weekly Girl Scout meeting where they discussed upcoming events and activities for their troop. Mrs. Sadrock didn't even mention the winners of the Girl Scout cookie challenge until the last few minutes of the meeting. Kayla and Pamela were on the edge of their seats in anticipation. When she announced the winners, Kayla and Pamela closed their eyes and crossed their fingers, hopeful that their names would be called.

"The recipients of the overnight camping trip from Troop 730 are......Kayla and Pamela!" Mrs. Sadrock announced.

The girls were so thrilled they began jumping up and down and shrieking in excitement. They were as loud as an elementary school lunch room. When Kayla's mom came to pick up her and Pamela, they couldn't wait to tell her all the details. The camping trip was only two days away and Kayla and Pamela were ready to go.

When Saturday morning arrived, Kayla and Pamela were both dressed in their most comfortable camping gear and were well equipped with everything they'd need to survive on the campgrounds for the weekend. Although they wouldn't be sleeping in tents, they knew they should be prepared for whatever came their way.

As they drove into Camp Hanover, the sweet smells of forest trees and plants filled the air. The open campsites, dirt paths, and picnic tables were some of the first sights they saw. As they settled into their cabin and began to unpack their things, Pamela screamed.

"It's not in here. I swear I packed it after I used it this morning! I even double checked my duffle bag before I left," cried Pamela.

"Relax, Pamela. Don't stress out. We'll find it," reassured Kayla.

"I'm so upset, Kayla!" wailed Pamela. "It's not like I can just run out and get a new one. We're in the middle of nowhere!"

Kayla was always calm. She never stressed out and always tried to see the bright side of things. She knew that if she didn't act confidently, Pamela would want to leave immediately.

"I have an idea," suggested Kayla. "Why don't we call the camp ranger since our chaperones aren't here? I bet he has an extra one in his office or something. Kids come here all the time and they know how important it is to have what you're missing," Kayla recommended.

Pamela immediately felt better. She knew Kayla was a great person to have with her on this camping trip. After Kayla phoned the camp ranger, he arrived with Pamela's missing item in a brand new plastic package. It wasn't pink like the one she used at home, but it would do. She was so happy that Kayla and the Camp Ranger came to the rescue.

"Now I don't have to worry about you using mine!" Kayla joked.

"Funny, Kayla. I know we're best friends, but I couldn't do that to you," replied Pamela.

1. Before the camping trip winners were announced, Kayla and Pamela felt
   A. nervous and pessimistic.
   B. confident and hopeful.
   C. angry and sad.
   D. unsure and hesitant.

2. What is Pamela's opinion of Kayla?
   A. She thinks that Kayla is too competitive.
   B. Kayla is not good in high-pressure situations.
   C. It's hard to be friends with Kayla.
   D. Kayla is helpful when Pamela is stressed.

3. The author mentioned the girls' ability to sell a lot of cookies to show the reader that they

    A. were strong, dependable leaders within their troop.

    B. weren't helpful in the community.

    C. enjoyed eating the cookies.

    D. enjoyed being in Junior Girl Scout Troop 730.

4. Pamela mentioned that she used her "missing item" the morning she left for the camping trip to imply that she

    A. rarely uses the item.

    B. needs the item on a daily basis.

    C. is an organized packer.

    D. doesn't remember the last time she saw it.

5. What information causes the reader to anticipate that something is going to go wrong?

    A. Pamela's description that they're in the middle of a campsite

    B. The fact that the girls are leaving on a Saturday morning

    C. Pamela's distress after unpacking her belongings

    D. Kayla's calm behavior

6. Using the clues from the reading, what do you predict the "missing item" is? Why was Pamela so upset about it not being packed in her bag for the long weekend? Cite examples from the text to support your answer.

_____

_____

_____

_____

_____

Exercise 3 Answers:

1. B

Kayla and Pamela felt confident and hopeful that they had won because they had worked hard to sell a lot of Girl Scout cookies for their troop. Letters A, C, and D are all opposites of what they were feeling.

2. D

Kayla is helpful when Pamela is stressed because she always stays calm under pressure. Answer A is not found in the reading passage, Answer B is the opposite of what the author explains about Kayla, and Answer C doesn't make sense for the reading passage.

3. A

By describing their average Girl Scout cookie sales, it proves that they were strong leaders within their troop.

4. B

The answer shows that Pamela needs the item she has forgotten on a daily basis and it implies that it is an important item to have for a weekend trip away.

5. C

The phrase, "Pamela screamed!" provides the reader with a mental picture that Pamela realized that she has forgotten something or not packed a necessary item.

6. Possible Answer: "As they settled into their cabin and began to unpack their things, Pamela screamed." When Kayla and Pamela were unpacking, Pamela noticed that something was missing from her duffle bag. Based on the details given, I would predict that Pamela is missing her toothbrush. Pamela was upset about not having it because she wanted to stay healthy and clean during her weekend trip. She also described that it was pink, which reminded me that toothbrushes come in a lot of different colors. When the camp ranger brought her item in a new, plastic case, I realized it was something that she would need to unwrap or open. When Pamela received her new item, she felt comfortable and at home.

Exercise 4: Making Inferences

Directions: Read the passage below and complete the activities that follow. Be sure to answer all parts of the question and support with evidence from the text, if necessary.

MISS McGILL'S MYSTERY

"The most important thing when writing a mystery is keeping up the suspense until the very last moment," Miss McGill revealed to our fifth grade class. "If you can do that, you'll have your readers second-guessing the suspect at every other page!"

Miss McGill was a mystery writer during her summers off. She enjoyed teaching writing techniques and often brought in stories she had written so we could understand the writing process fully. It wasn't a secret that mystery was her favorite writing genre. She'd bring in props and have us act out certain scenes to intensify what it's really like when looking for clues and suspects.

On Tuesday night, she gave us a homework assignment that required that we read clues from a mystery case file and come up with our own conclusions about who did it and their motives. Everyone in Miss McGill's class was so wound up about their homework assignment that they ran home without stopping to ensure they had enough time to crack the case. On their walk home, Joshua and Sal talked about the assignment.

"OUCH!" screamed Joshua as he ran right into the fire hydrant. Everything was blurry and he could barely see! Joshua realized he forgot his glasses at school, so he turned around and started to head back. "Don't worry about me, Sal. You should go home and get started on the case." Joshua knew he wouldn't be able to do his work without his glasses and didn't think it was fair to make Sal accompany him back to school because of his mistake.

When Joshua returned to school, Miss McGill was on her way out the door.

"I just need to grab my glasses, Miss McGill," Joshua stated.

"Not a problem, Joshua. Be careful, I know how you are when you don't have your glasses!" reminded Miss McGill. As she walked away, she knew that tomorrow the kids would be left with a great mystery to solve.

The next morning, as some of Miss McGill's class entered the room, they noticed their disheveled classroom and their teacher was missing. Their classroom looked like a crime scene complete with desks toppled over, homework sprawled across the green tiled floor, and a manila envelope sitting atop a stool at the front of the room.

"Where is Miss McGill?" questioned Nate. "I hope nothing bad happened to her. Maybe she's sick."

"That's not what the evidence suggests," Martin argued. He was always going against what everyone else thought. Maybe he liked to be persnickety.

When the others made their way into the classroom, it became clear to the students that something had happened, but they were unsure of the when, how, and why. Being the responsible students that they were, they called the office to report that they did not have a teacher. Then, just like a sly fox, Principal Gladstone waltzed through the door.

"What seems to be the . . . oh! What happened here last night?" Principal Gladstone inquired.

"Miss McGill is absent today, Mr. Gladstone. We think something terrible happened here last night," cried Emma. Emma was overly dramatic and a bit peculiar. Miss McGill had told her that if she used some of that drama in her writing, she'd be famous someday.

"Yes, I've spoken to her already — I mean, well, what's the first thing we should do?" he stuttered.

Martin happily pointed out the manila envelope resting quite nicely on the stool in the front of the room. "A CLUE!" yelled Martin. Everyone huddled around the stool like a bunch of football players setting up for their next play.

"I'm going to leave you guys to solve this mystery. I will be back within the hour," Mr. Gladstone said confidently. As he walked out, they began to think of all the possible reasons for the messy classroom. They began to notice the little things first.

"The toppled-over desks suggests that maybe our suspect was looking for something," Jessica inferred.

"And the closet doors are open! Miss McGill always makes sure they're shut before she leaves," Nate chimed in. "I'm thinking the suspect thought he could find what he was looking for in there, too."

As the children sat around, Martin examined the manila envelope. "Hey guys, come check this out!" he yelled. "This folder has all our math tests from yesterday. They're in alphabetical order. Maybe we should look to see if any are missing." One by one, Martin checked the math tests, but they were all there. Not one math test was out of order.

"Looks like we've reached a dead end," insisted Joshua.

Underneath the math tests, on a small sheet of yellow lined paper lay a note from the school nurse. It read, "Please make sure Joshua takes his glasses home each night and brings them back to school each day. Without them, he can barely see what's in front of him." Sal swiftly snatched the note from the folder. He suddenly remembered his and Joshua's walk home yesterday and realized what had happened.

"I know exactly who did it and I'll explain it to you all once you've taken a seat," Sal said proudly.

1. Using the information from the passage, who do you think Sal accuses of being the suspect? Explain your answer.

_____

_____

_____

_____

_____

2. Why do you think the manila envelope was placed on the stool for the students to find?

_____

_____

_____

_____

_____

_____

3. In your opinion, do you think the "suspect" should get in trouble? Why or why not? Use examples from the passage to support your answer.

_____

_____

_____

_____

_____

_____

4. Based on how the story ends, predict what you think Miss McGill would say when she returned to school.

_____

_____

_____

_____

_____

_____

5. Why do you think the author provides us with details about Joshua and Sal's walk home? Explain.

_____

_____

_____

_____

_____

_____

6. In your opinion, why do you think Principal Gladstone left the students alone to solve the mystery?

_____

_____

_____

_____

_____

Exercise 4 Answers:

RESPONSES MAY VARY

1. Sal would accuse Joshua of being the suspect because he was with Joshua on the walk home when Joshua ran into the fire hydrant and admitted he couldn't see without his glasses. Sal also knew that Joshua went back to school to get his glasses. After he found the note from the nurse, Sal knew it must have been Joshua.

2. The manila envelope was placed on the stool for the students to find so they would pick up the envelope, look through it, and eventually find the note from the nurse.

3. Possible Answer: I don't think the suspect should get in trouble because clearly, if it was Joshua, he couldn't see because he didn't have his glasses on. As he was trying to find his glasses, he knocked over a bunch of things. Maybe he thought he was going to get in trouble and thought it would just be best to leave before anyone saw him and thought he did it on purpose.

4. Possible Answer: I think Miss McGill would have said, "I should've stayed when Joshua was looking for his glasses," because he made such a big mess and she knew he couldn't see without them. I also think she probably would have congratulated her class on the way they handled the "crime scene." She would be very proud of them.

5. Possible Answer: I think the author provided us with many details about Sal and Joshua's walk home to clue us in that something might happen when Joshua returned to school.

6. Possible Answer: I think that Principal Gladstone left the students to solve the crime on their own because he had already spoken with Miss McGill and she had asked him to try and have them piece together the clues. Another reason could be that Mr. Gladstone had seen Joshua leaving school that day. Since he knew Miss McGill would be absent the next day, he checked to make sure her plans for the substitute teacher were ready and he would have seen the mess.

MAIN IDEA AND SUPPORTING DETAILS

The **main idea** tells you what the story is about. It is the most important part of a story or paragraph. The **supporting details** help to guide you towards locating the main idea. The more supporting details you add, the richer your paragraph will be. They also makes the main idea more evident or clear to the reader.

Without a main idea and supporting details, any story you read won't make much sense. It wouldn't have a clear focus, and it would be hard for you to follow and answer questions about what you've just read. The topic sentence of any paragraph should clue you into the theme or main idea of that paragraph. Usually, a change in paragraph means a change in an idea, topic, or concept.

You will also need to do a bit of making **inferences** and drawing **conclusions**. Connect what you already know to what you're about to read. Make predictions, evaluate, and interpret what the author provides for you. Many times, it will be up to you to read the details carefully and connect them to what you comprehend.

Main Idea Tips

Here are a few tips to follow when trying to locate the main idea of a written piece:

* What is the topic of the story?

* Locate details that describe events, characters, or problem and solution.

* The last paragraph is often used to briefly restate the central ideas of the story.

At the end of the reading ask yourself, "What was the subject of this writing? What details support my conclusion? Can I summarize in my own words what happened?" If you can't answer all three of these questions, you haven't grasped the key concepts of the subject matter.

Exercise 5: Main Idea and Supporting Details

Directions: Read the passage below and complete the activities that follow. Be sure to answer all parts of the question and support with evidence from the text, if necessary.

BUSY BEES

 "Mmmm…Honey!" Ever wonder why your flowers always look so pretty in the summertime? How about where honey comes from? You can thank the bees for both of these things! Bees are very useful to humans and are tremendously fascinating insects. There are over 4,000 different kinds in the United States alone; however, the honeybee seems to be the most popular and well-known.

The honey bee is quite the active insect. It has been around for millions of years and is the only insect that produces food that humans consume. An average beehive ranges from 40,000-80,000 bees at one time. That's a lot of bees working in one place! They fly up to 15 miles an hour and communicate with other honey bees by engaging in a form of "dancing." During pollination trips, honey bees travel among 50-100 flowers picking up sweet nectar (which flowers produce) along the way. Once they've collected their nectar, honey bees travel back to their hives to deposit and store it. Eventually, it evaporates into what we humans know as honey.

"May I have another spoonful, please?" Honey isn't just a tasty treat for us to enjoy. Humans use honey for many different purposes. Humans often use honey in their cooking because it is a natural sugar substitute. Many people recommend using honey as a natural remedy to help cure rashes and even allergies. Some scientists even proclaim that using honey as a beauty product will make your skin soft and your hair shiny! Learning about all these benefits that honey offers urges humans to preserve, respect, and appreciate the honeybees that populate the United States!

1. The main idea of the entire passage is to teach readers about
   A. the population of honeybees.
   B. how honeybees communicate with each other.
   C. how delicious honey is.
   D. the various ways in which honeybees can be useful to humans.

2. All of the following are examples of supporting details in paragraph 2 EXCEPT

   A. There are over 4,000 different kinds in the United States alone.

   B. They fly up to 15 mph and communicate with other honeybees by "dancing."

   C. Honeybees travel among 50-100 flowers (which produce nectar).

   D. The honeybee is the only insect that produces food that humans consume.

3. The main idea of the third paragraph is that

   A. honey is extremely tasty.

   B. honey is used by humans in a variety of ways.

   C. honey is a natural sweetener used in place of sugar.

   D. honeybees are overpopulating the United States.

4. The concluding sentence of paragraph 3 urges readers to

   A. help catch the honeybees while they're pollinating.

   B. try using honey in their hair to make it shiny.

   C. help preserve the honeybees in the United States.

   D. use honey when they have allergies.

5. The author provides the detail "an average beehive ranges from 40,000-80,000 bees at one time" to illustrate that

   A. bees are constantly working and sharing space.

   B. they have big families.

   C. they are under-populated.

   D. bees don't like living together.

6. Summarize the supporting details that explain how honey is made.

_____

_____

_____

_____

_____

Exercise 5 Answers:

1. **D**

   The author's main idea in this passage is to teach readers about the various ways in which honeybees are useful to humans. Although choices A, B, and C all appear somewhere in the passage, they are supporting details to the main idea.

2. **A**

   The example, "there are 4,000 different kinds in the United States alone" appears in paragraph 1.

3. **B**

   "Honey is used by humans in a variety of ways" is the best choice for the main idea of paragraph 3. Choice A is an opinion. Choice C is a fact but isn't the main idea of the paragraph. Choice D should have been crossed out immediately because it is not found in the passage.

4. **C**

   The concluding sentence in paragraph 3 persuades us to take action and help preserve the honeybees in the United States. Choices A, B, and D do not influence us to take action.

5. **A**

   The author provides us with a detail about the amount of honeybees in a hive to illustrate that they are constantly working together. Choices B, C, and D are not supporting details of the example sentence.

6. **Possible Answer:** "Buzz!" That's the sound of bees traveling from flower to flower. When bees pollinate, they make what humans enjoy as honey. They receive nectar from flowers and head back to their hives to store it. Eventually, it evaporates and turns to honey. Honey is great for a variety of things, too. Some scientists claim it can make your skin soft and help ease the pain of some allergies. Bees are very helpful to humans. Without them, we'd have no honey!

Exercise 6: Main Idea and Supporting Details

Directions: Read the passage below and complete the activities that follow. Be sure to answer all parts of the question and support with evidence from the text, if necessary.

CHECKMATE!

What is chess all about, anyway? If you consider it "just a game" you are wrong. Most chess players would argue that chess is a historic pastime which involves a two-player challenge of intelligence and strategy.

"Let's battle!" Chess players often choose an equally-matched opponent so that the game is not only fair, but also a complete battle of the minds. Many spectators believe that chess is a difficult game, but avid chess players disagree. Chess requires you to think abstractly and have the cleverness to outsmart your opponent. This makes it one of the most sought–after competitions to study. There are millions of variations on how the game may unfold, which makes the appeal of winning a chess game a great triumph.

"Tick, Tock, Tick, Tock," goes the chess clock. Several chess players spend years mastering the sport. Oftentimes, players try and predict several moves ahead of where their opponent may play and base their strategy around one small possibility. Patience and technique is vital in maintaining competitive play. In chess, you can't cheat or win on luck alone. The strategy to win chess is a bit more complex; train, practice, and carry out the task to outwit your opponent. Capture your opponent's King and you have a win under your belt.

Checkmate! The creative element to chess is what makes the game so special to its players. As with any competition, one must be prepared for whatever is thrown his way. Even though there are many rules in chess, being creative and thinking outside the box could prove to be beneficial. Sometimes, taking a risk pays off. Other times, the best offense is a great defense. This game is not for the faint of heart. As with many pastimes, although it provides entertainment for many, players are physically, passionately, and emotionally invested in every aspect in the pursuit of victory.

1. What is the main idea of this passage?

_____

_____

_____

_____

_____

2. What is the main idea of paragraph 2? Describe the supporting details to show this.

_____

_____

_____

_____

_____

3. What is the main idea of paragraph 3? Describe the supporting details to show this.

_____

_____

_____

_____

_____

4. What is the main idea of paragraph 4? Describe the supporting details to show this.

_____

_____

_____

_____

_____

_____

5. Using details from the passage, what is the most important skill when learning to play chess?

_____

_____

_____

_____

_____

_____

Exercise 6 Answers:

1. The main idea of this passage is that chess is a game of mind and strategy.

2. The main idea of paragraph 2 tells the reader a few facts about chess. In the paragraph it says that you need to think abstractly and use cleverness to be a good chess player.

3. The main idea of paragraph 3 is all about strategy. It explains how players think and move their pieces.

4. The main idea of paragraph 4 is what makes chess so appealing to its players. It provides examples of how creative players get and how much they put into winning the game. The ultimate goal is a victory and the author uses that idea in the last paragraph to wrap up the passage.

5. The most important skill when learning to play chess is strategy. Predicting your opponent's moves and outcomes will help you organize a plan of attack and anticipate your next move.

AUTHOR'S PURPOSE

Understanding the author's purpose will also help you identify the main idea and most important details when reading a passage or story. When authors sit down to write a story, they usually think to themselves, "Do I want to inform, entertain, or persuade my audience?" Asking this question allows authors to establish what type of audience they would like to reach. Sometimes, authors may have more than one purpose or audience. When you can identify the author's purpose, you will have a better understanding about what you are reading.

Use the following chart to help you establish the author's purpose for writing:

To Inform:	Who, Where, When, What, Why, How
To Entertain:	Characters, Setting, Problem, Events, Solution
To Persuade:	Audience, Point of view, Supporting reasons

Exercise 7: Author's Purpose

Directions: Read the following passages. Describe whether the author is trying to inform, entertain, or persuade his/her reader. Provide examples when necessary.

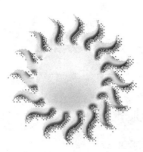

(a) Where would we be without the Sun? Not only is the Sun a star, it is the center of our Solar System and over five billion years old! Although it is 93 million miles from Earth, it takes just over eight minutes for the Sun's light to reach Earth. Sunlight of course, travels at the speed of light. The Sun has been exploding for billions of years and generates heat from its core. Humans rely on the Sun's heat, energy, and light to survive. Without the Sun, Earth would be unable to support any kind of life.

Clocking in at twenty-seven million degrees Fahrenheit makes it hard for scientists to get close to the Sun; however, modern technology has made it easier for scientists to capture images. Using telescopes, scientists are able to study solar winds and sunspots, and predict patterns in the Sun's activity, all of which ultimately affects the climate on Earth. Unfortunately the Sun will burn out, but not to worry; it is predicted to shine for another four billion years.

The Author's Purpose for writing this passage was to . . . (circle one)

Inform   **Entertain**   **Persuade**

What evidence from the text demonstrates the Author's Purpose?

_____

_____

_____

_____

_____

(b) Parents are beginning to think their children are spending too much time using technology. Young people are craving their electronic devices now, more than ever, since laptops, notebooks, iPods, and cell phones have become popular. Don't you agree that technology is making youngsters lazier?

Young people enjoy the entertainment that technology provides. Children of all ages are opting to text their friends or use social media instead of reading a book or doing their homework. They think technology is the best invention of the past decade. If young people don't put away their technology now it may be too late. Since most children from the ages of 8-18 spend more than seven hours a day on these gadgets, families aren't able to spend quality time together. Youngsters are even losing interest in sports, other activities, and physical exercise. They need to leave the technology at home and get out and be active. They'll be happier, fit, and totally focused. Too much tech is too much!

The Author's Purpose for writing this passage is to . . . (circle one)

Inform   **Entertain**   **Persuade**

What evidence from the text demonstrates the Author's Purpose?

_____

_____

_____

_____

_____

(c) It was a beautiful, spring day when my friend James and I went outside to play. Little did we know we were in for a real adventure. From the moment I stepped outside my door, I knew something was different. I looked to the left, I looked to the right, and there it was. When James came over, he was out of breath and red in the face. He had noticed it too. When he finally calmed down, we both grabbed our bicycles and rode down the street. When we got close to it, we could see that it was the most fascinating sight we had ever seen.

The Author's Purpose for writing this passage was to . . . (circle one)

Inform   **Entertain**   **Persuade**

What evidence from the text demonstrates the Author's Purpose?

_____

_____

_____

_____

_____

_____

 Now that you have read some ways to inform, entertain, and persuade readers, try the following sentences. Read the descriptions below and determine the author's purpose in writing them (to **inform, entertain,** or **persuade**). Then, explain what literary elements helped you decide on your answer.

1. A family of five decided to travel cross-country on a road trip. On their way, they realized they had forgotten to complete an important task at home before they left.

   Author's Purpose: _____

   Explanation:

   _____

   _____

   _____

   _____

   _____

   _____

2. The principal has taken away your privilege of sitting with your friends at lunchtime. Your teacher encourages you to voice your opinion and write a letter explaining why you believe it's important to have that privilege at lunch.

   Author's Purpose: _____

   Explanation:

   _____

   _____

   _____

   _____

   _____

   _____

3. The school nurse is holding a meeting to discuss ways children can deal with stress, bullying, and social issues. Your parents are also invited to attend.

Author's Purpose: _____

Explanation:

_____

_____

_____

_____

_____

_____

4. On the day of a big test, Amy walks in and tells Julie she hasn't studied for it. She confides to Julie that she's going to cheat by looking at Brian's test to make sure she passes. After the test, Julie decides that telling the teacher what Amy did is the right choice. The teacher calls Amy's parents and requests a meeting to discuss the incident.

Author's Purpose: _____

Explanation:

_____

_____

_____

_____

_____

5. Spencer arrives home from school one day and is greeted by his parents, who hand him a special package. As he tears into the gift, he screams with excitement.

Author's Purpose: _____

Explanation:

_____

_____

_____

_____

_____

_____

6. Andrew is giving an oral report on why students should be able to wear hats in school. He provides relevant facts and a poll of his classmates' opinions. At the end of his report, his teacher allows the students to wear hats in class.

Author's Purpose: _____

Explanation:

_____

_____

_____

_____

_____

_____

Exercise 7 Answers:

a. The author's purpose for writing this passage was to **inform** readers. The evidence from the text demonstrates the author's purpose was to inform readers about the importance of the Sun to human life on Earth. It also provided facts about the Sun's atmosphere and how scientists use images of the Sun to predict patterns that can affect the Earth.

b. The author's purpose for writing this passage was to **persuade** readers. The evidence from the text demonstrates the author's purpose was to persuade by presenting facts and opinions about technology and the effect it has on children from 8-18. It also provided alternatives to using technology and urged young people to get out and be active instead.

c. The author's purpose for writing this passage was to **entertain** readers. The evidence from the text demonstrates the author's purpose was to entertain readers by creating suspense about a "fascinating sight." The author never explained what the sight was, challenging the readers to read on or to use their own imaginations.

1. **Author's Purpose:** Entertain

   Explanation: The author is trying to hook readers by creating a slight problem in the family's road trip. Since the task they forgot to do isn't mentioned, it allows the readers to come up with solutions of their own.

2. **Author's Purpose:** Persuade

   Explanation: The author is using the principal as someone who is enforcing a rule and taking away a privilege. When the teacher suggests that you "voice your opinion" by writing a letter, we can assume you are going to provide facts and opinions about the topic and the principal's decision.

3. **Author's Purpose:** Inform

   Explanation: The author is providing a situation in which students and parents can come and listen to the school nurse talk about various topics relating to their families. Stress, bullying, and social issues can be dealt with by using strategies and devising a plan, all of which will be introduced by the school nurse.

4. Author's Purpose: Inform

Explanation: The author is creating a scenario in which one friend knows that the other is doing the wrong thing. In this passage, Julie does the right thing by telling the teacher. The author tries to teach the reader that it's always better to do the right thing, even if the offender is your friend.

5. Author's Purpose: Entertain

Explanation: Once again, the author is trying to hook the reader by introducing a "special package" whose contents are unknown to the reader. It also illustrates to the reader that the boy receiving the package is excited and eager to find out what's inside.

6. Author's Purpose: Persuade

Explanation: The author is using Andrew as a student who is trying to persuade his teacher to allow hats in class. Since Andrew has polled his class on their opinions, it hints to the reader that he has built an argument and used facts to make an effective statement.

CONTEXT CLUES

Context clues are **hints** in a sentence or paragraph that the author provides to help the reader understand the meaning of new vocabulary words. Presenting the hints *before* or *after* the new word provides you with tools needed to build upon your current vocabulary.

As a reader, you must be aware that some words have multiple meanings. Using the clues in the sentence will help you choose the best definition in the appropriate context. Often, students know the definition of the word prior to reading it; however, a question will ask you what it means in that specific paragraph, which may be used in a different context. Even though a dictionary is a great resource, it may not always be readily available. On a standardized test, you will have to rely on the hints the author provides to guide you to the right answer.

Exercise 8: Context Clues

Directions: Locate the bold word in each sentence and use the clues before and after to help you decide on the meaning. You may want to underline the clues to help form your definition.

1. As we began to copy down our spelling words, our teacher told us to write **meticulously** so we wouldn't make any mistakes.

   Your definition: _____

2. The public library had a **vast** selection of library books to choose from when writing my report on jungle animals.

   Your definition: _____

3. After a long morning of math and an intense football game, I was **famished** and ready for lunch!

   Your definition: _____

4. My mother told me I was acting a bit **haughty** when I complained of having nothing to wear, when I had a closet full of options.

   Your definition: _____

5. My father had an **incredulous** smile on his face when I told him my class went on a field trip to outer space.

   Your definition: _____

Exercise 8 Answers:

1. **Meticulously; carefully, concerned with detail**

   When the teacher used the word **meticulously**, it was followed by the words **so we wouldn't make any mistakes** indicating they should pay close attention to detail and neatness.

2. **Vast; Very great in size, amount**

   The setting of the library indicates there are many books to choose from and a wide range in a variety of topics.

3. **Famished; extremely hungry**

   The context clue of a math lesson and a football game indicates the person speaking was working very hard and worked up an appetite. The word **lunch** also helped when defining the word.

4. **Haughty; having or showing arrogance**

   The person speaking had a closet full of clothes; therefore, her mother insisted that she was acting conceited, or stuck up, when complaining about her lack of options.

5. **Incredulous; disbelieving**

   When the speaker told her father she went on a trip to outer space, the father's smile showed he did not believe her.

Exercise 9: Context Clues

Directions: Read the following passage and answer the following questions. Use examples from the passage to support your response.

APPLE PICKING

As Julia's summer vacation was nearing an end, she had a sudden urge to go on one more adventurous day trip with her mom. Apple picking was at the top of her list for a **plethora** of reasons. Julia had never been to an apple orchard and apples were one of her most favorite fruits. She also knew that summer was the best time to pick ripe, bright, and juicy apples.

"Variety is the spice of life!" sang Julia's mom as they hopped in the car and headed towards Alan's Apple Orchard. "I printed out a few tips for us to follow when we arrive at the orchard. Why don't you read these over while we drive?" she asked.

"Apple picking is all about variety," Julia read, understanding her mom's silly song earlier. "It's important to choose what you'd like to use your apples for before picking them. Who knew there were that many ways to use apples?" Julia questioned.

"What should our **objective** be? Pie filling, cider, jam, jelly, applesauce, storing?" posed Julia's mom. She was always organized and liked to have a plan in mind.

"Let's make applesauce, Mom! It'd be the perfect back-to-school snack, and we can store what we don't use!" Julia exclaimed.

Upon arriving, Julia and her mother were greeted by a pleasant and **affable** farmer dressed in blue jean overalls and a bright smile. He offered to give them a tour of the orchard and assist them in their apple-picking **endeavor**. On their walk, he rattled off several interesting facts about apples, such as, "It takes about 36 apples to create one gallon of apple cider," and "2,500 varieties of apples are grown in the United States." He seemed quite knowledgeable on the subject.

When their baskets were full, John the farmer gave them a few important tips that would help them prepare a tasty batch of applesauce.

"Don't wash them until right before you use them, to prevent spoiling, and keep them in a cool place to maintain that juicy flavor," he instructed.

On the drive home, Julia and her mother slipped their hands into their **bountiful** basket and picked an apple to eat. Julia hoped that this trip would become a tradition every year before school started up again.

1. In the first paragraph, the word **plethora** means
   A. shortage.
   B. a lot of.
   C. extra.
   D. lacking.

2. In the passage, the word **objective** means all of the following EXCEPT
   A. purpose.
   B. goal.
   C. intention.
   D. unfair.

3. In the sentence, "Upon arrival, Julia and her mother were greeted by a pleasant and **affable** farmer," the word **affable** means
   A. terrifying.
   B. unwelcoming.
   C. friendly.
   D. comical.

4. In the passage, the word **endeavor** means
   A. mission.
   B. offering.
   C. contribution.
   D. pattern.

5. An antonym for the word **bountiful**, found in the last paragraph, would be

   A. plentiful.

   B. empty.

   C. overflowing.

   D. full.

6. Imagine that you went apple picking with someone in your family. What would you choose to make before you filled your basket with apples? Explain your choice.

_____

_____

_____

_____

_____

_____

Exercise 9 Answers:

1. **B**

   Choices A and D are opposites of the bold word, and choice C means having more than needed.

2. **D**

   Choices A, B, and C are synonyms for the word **objective**.

3. **C**

   The word **pleasant** was a hint that **affable** meant friendly or welcoming. Choices A and B are antonyms and choice D wasn't described.

4. **A**

   If you plug in letter choices B, C, or D, the sentence does not make sense.

5. **D**

   Empty would be the opposite of **bountiful. Plentiful, overflowing** and **full** are all synonyms for bountiful.

6. **Possible Answer:** "Apple pie, yum!" Whenever I hear the words "apple pie," my mouth begins to water. If I went apple picking with my mom, we would have used the shiny, red, juicy apples to make an apple pie for our family to enjoy. My family thinks that dessert is the best part of the meal! Apple pie is delicious and best served with vanilla ice cream. A great dessert is not complete without a cold glass of milk to wash it down. Another slice, please!

ANALYZING TEXT

 Now that you've had some practice with reading comprehension and literary elements, analyzing text will further assist you in applying information and using critical thinking strategies. In this section, you will practice evaluating text, determine the importance of information, answer essential questions, and sort and classify ideas into their component parts.

Analyzing text will require you to take a closer look at the information being presented. As you become better readers, you will be able to find new meanings through analysis and reflection. You'll be able to craft your own ideas and experience a variety of text structures.

It is important to know the order or sequence of events that takes place in a story.

A few skills you'll be observing in this section are as follows:

Compare/Contrast	Authors use comparisons to describe ideas to readers. Similes, metaphors, and analogies are used in compare/contrast structures.
Cause/Effect	Informational texts often describe cause and effect relationships. Cause and effect analysis is an attempt to understand why things happen as they do. The text describes events and identifies or suggests possible causes and factors for situations.
Sequence	(Time/Order) Chronological articles and text reveal events in a sequence from beginning to end. Words that signal chronological structures include: **first, then, next, finally,** and specific dates and times.

Exercise 10: Sequencing

Directions: Read the following passage and answer the questions that follow. Look for signal words like **first**, **next**, **last**, **before**, **after** and **finally** to sequence the order of events.

PARTY TIME

 Matthew's 12th birthday was quickly approaching and he had a ton of party planning to do with his dad. He was determined to plan the best birthday party ever. First, Matthew and his dad made a list of all the necessary items needed for the party. These included plates, forks, spoons, decorations and, most importantly, party favors. Just then, Matthew realized that one small thing was missing: a theme.

"What type of birthday party do you want to have, Matthew?" questioned his dad.

"I was thinking of a rock–climbing party. I did some research online and found out that we could rent a rock-climbing wall. All we'd need to do is make sure there is a trained professional to spot us," said Matthew assertively.

"Fantastic! I'll go make the call and reserve the date now," his dad remarked.

The following days were filled with excitement. Next, Matthew and his father designed the invitation that they would send out to all of Matthew's friends and family. After careful consideration, Matthew and his father agreed that he could invite 10 of his friends to his birthday party, but that they would need to get their parents' permission to climb the wall. Matthew felt that was fair and decided it would be good information to include on the invite, as well.

After the invitations went out, Matthew waited patiently for the RSVPs. All ten of his friends were able to make it! He was thrilled. All that was left to do was order a delicious cake.

"Hi, my name is Matthew, and I'd like to place an order for a chocolate and vanilla ice-cream cake. Is it possible for that to be three tiers? I'll need it ready for pick–up by tomorrow at noon. Thanks!" requested Matthew.

The day of the party arrived. Matthew's friends were dressed and ready to scale the rock-climbing wall. After they worked up an appetite, they snacked on hot dogs and potato chips. When it was time for Matthew to blow out the candles, everyone remarked how scrumptious the cake looked. Matthew took great pride, knowing that he had planned a great birthday party that all of his friends would never forget.

1. The first thing that Matthew did to plan his party was to
   A. call his friends to see if they could make it.
   B. make a list of everything he needed for his party.
   C. call and reserve the rock-climbing wall.
   D. create an invitation.

2. Matthew and his father decided the next step in planning the party was to
   A. pick a theme for the party.
   B. order a cake.
   C. snack on hot dogs.
   D. call parents to see if they could chaperone.

3. After Matthew and his father designed the invite, they
   A. ordered the cake.
   B. bought party favors.
   C. waited for the guests to RSVP.
   D. sent the invitation to 10 of Matthew's friends.

4. The last preparation Matthew needed to make was to
   A. get rock-climbing shoes.
   B. pack the party favors.
   C. order the ice-cream cake.
   D. string the party lights.

5. When the day of the party arrived,
   A. Matthew knew he had planned a great party.
   B. none of his friends came.
   C. Matthew's dad forgot to pick up the cake.
   D. Matthew couldn't believe how big the rock-climbing wall was.

6. Based on the information given in the last paragraph, what would be the next reasonable event that could have happened after Matthew and his friends ate birthday cake? Explain.

_____

_____

_____

_____

_____

_____

Exercise 10 Answers:

1. **B**

   Matthew needed to make a list of everything they'd need so they could begin to plan his party.

2. **A**

   Before Matthew could plan his party, his dad suggested they come up with a theme for the party. Choices B, C, and D come later in the passage.

3. **D**

   Although choice C is tempting, it jumps too far ahead and skips over Matthew sending out the invitations to his friends. Choice A comes later in the passage, and answer choice B was not mentioned.

4. **C**

   Matthew called himself to order the cake. Answer choices A, B, and D were not logical choices or mentioned in the story.

5. **A**

   The correct choice is A. Matthew mentioned earlier in the passage that he wanted to plan a birthday party that everyone would enjoy. Choices B, C, and D are all opposites of what happened last in the passage.

6. **Possible Answer**: After Matthew and his friends enjoyed the birthday cake, they would most likely play a little bit at Matthew's house and then receive goody bags before they left. They would also use good manners and thank Matthew and his parents for having them at his birthday party.

Exercise 11: Compare/Contrast

Directions: Read the following passage and answer the questions that follow.

CRUISE SHIP VACATION

 This winter my family decided to escape the cold and celebrate the holidays on a cruise ship. Warm sun, green oceans, and planned adventures were just what we needed after a cold and bitter winter.

Normally, our vacations were all the same. We would take two weeks in the summer because everyone is off from school. My dad works a lot and says the summertime is easier for him to be away from the office. Mom always coordinates the trip and makes sure we have fun activities planned and full suitcases packed for a trip to the beach.

This cruise lasted eight days and we sailed all around the Caribbean. We made a ton of stops in local towns and visited boutiques and farm stands. It was a bit more exhausting than our normal vacations of lying on the beach, flying kites, and playing beach volleyball.

During the day, our family was very productive. We tried our best to soak up as much of the culture as we could. We visited tourist attractions and explored historical landmarks. At night, we spent a lot of time as a family eating dinner, playing card games, and attending a few shows and performances on the ship. No matter where we took a vacation, we always ended up playing card games together. My family is so competitive!

Those eight days flew by. Spending the holidays on a cruise ship sure was fun, but we all began to miss the traditions of spending them at home. There was no snow or special baked goods to devour. We didn't open presents or sing holiday songs. As the sadness settled in, we all agreed that we should stick to our normal, two-week summer vacation next year.

When we arrived home after a five-hour plane ride, everyone was exhausted. We were not used to such long travels; our beach vacations had been only two hours away! We pulled up to our house, snow-covered and decorated with icicles and colored lights. We pushed open the front door and immediately ran to our presents and settled in nicely while Mom put on a pot of hot cocoa. We were frozen down to our bones, but we couldn't have been happier to be home.

1. Describe why the family usually planned a vacation during the summer.

_____

_____

_____

_____

_____

_____

2. Compare and contrast the family's two vacations. How were they alike and different?

_____

_____

_____

_____

_____

_____

3. How were the activities they participated in on the cruise ship different from their beach activities? Provide one example.

_____

_____

_____

_____

_____

_____

4. Describe what the family did at night on the cruise ship. Was this similar or different from how they normally spent their vacation evenings? Explain.

_____

_____

_____

_____

_____

_____

5. Why did the kids prefer to have the holidays at home?

_____

_____

_____

_____

_____

6. Compare and contrast a vacation you've taken to the one in the story. How are they the same and different? Explain.

_____

_____

_____

_____

_____

Exercise 11: Answers:

1. The family usually planned a vacation in the summer because school was not in session. It was also easier for their dad to take time off during the less busy summer months.

2. The family in the passage enjoyed taking vacations together. Although the vacations were in different places, such as a cruise ship and a beach, they also shared a lot of the same qualities. One way that the vacations were different was that instead of going in the summertime, they went over their winter vacation. Also, one vacation was on a ship while others were at the beach. Another way in which they were similar was that they still did activities and ate dinner together as a family.

3. The activities that the family participated in on the cruise ship were different from their beach activities in several ways. On the cruise ship, they stopped in local towns and saw historical sites. On their beach trip, they played beach volleyball and relaxed.

4. The family in the passage spent all of their nights together. They normally ate dinner as a family, played cards, or caught a show or performance that the cruise ship provided. It was very similar to their activities when they took a beach vacation because they enjoyed spending time together.

5. The kids in the story preferred to have their holidays at home rather than on the cruise ship because they missed baking cookies and singing holiday songs. Being in warm weather made them miss a lot of the things they associated with the holiday, such as snow and lights and presents!

6. **Possible Answer:** "Hey, wait up!" I screamed to my brother as he was running towards the ocean. I love taking beach vacations with my family. We have a house in South Carolina and go every summer to relax and unwind. One way my vacation is similar to the one in the passage is that we also go during the summertime. It's when we're out of school and also when my dad can take off from his photography business. One way our vacations are different is that my family goes out to dinner every night, and we usually have a volleyball or soccer game on the beach after dinner. I love summer vacations!

Exercise 12: Cause/Effect

Directions: Read the following statements and identify the cause and effect for each.

> **Example:** Today I was late to school because I forgot to set my alarm clock.
>
> **Cause:** I forgot to set my alarm clock.
>
> **Effect:** I was late to school.

1. My class had wonderful behavior so our teacher gave us a night with no homework.

Cause:

Effect:

2. Brad couldn't play in the soccer game because he didn't wear cleats.

Cause:

Effect:

3. Joni saved her allowance to buy a dress from her favorite store.

Cause:

Effect:

4. Blair and Jenny were very thirsty after running three miles around the park.

Cause:

Effect:

5. When John got into college, he moved four states away from his family.

Cause:

Effect:

6. We ran out of cold cereal so we had to eat oatmeal instead.

Cause:

Effect:

Exercise 12: Answers:

1. My class had wonderful behavior so our teacher gave us a night of no homework.

   Cause: My class had wonderful behavior.

   Effect: My teacher gave them a night with no homework.

2. Brad couldn't play in the soccer game because he didn't wear cleats.

   Cause: Brad didn't wear cleats.

   Effect: He couldn't play in the soccer game.

3. Joni saved her allowance to buy a dress from her favorite store.

   Cause: Joni saved her allowance.

   Effect: She was able to buy a dress from her favorite store.

4. Blair and Jenny were very thirsty after running three miles around the park.

   Cause: Blair and Jenny ran three miles around the part.

   Effect: They were very thirsty.

5. When John got into college, he moved four states away from his family.

   Cause: John got into college.

   Effect: He moved four states away from his family.

6. We ran out of cold cereal so we had to eat oatmeal instead.

   Cause: We ran out of cold cereal.

   Effect: We had to eat oatmeal instead.

Chapter 3 Writing Prompts

The NJ ASK test for Grade 5 requires you to respond to expository and speculative writing prompts. You will be given 30 minutes to write a full essay that reflects the question(s) in the prompt.

This chapter focuses on the tools you'll need to complete the writing task in the time allotted. Useful hints, skills practice, and writing exercises will help prepare you for the timed writing portion of the Language Arts Literacy Test. Good luck and happy writing!

Keep the following in mind as you are working through this section:

Keep Track of Time: Keeping an eye on the clock will help you monitor where you are in your writing. If you spend five minutes prewriting and planning, you'll know how much time you need to complete the writing task. It's also helpful to leave a few minutes at the end to revise and review the work you've just written. Keeping track of time is not meant to scare you; it just provides a framework in which you can work.

Follow Directions: It's important that you use the prompt to answer the questions. Carefully rereading the prompt allows you to accurately answer each part in detail. For example, if the prompt asks you to write about you and your family, you'll want to make sure you provide examples of things that you and your family members do together. For speculative writing, you may be asked to write about a girl named Kara and an adventure she's been on. You'll want to make sure you write about a girl, not a boy! These are simple tips for you to be successful in your timed writing.

Do Your Best: It's hard to be proud of a writing piece when you only have 30 minutes, but as long as you focus on your essay and keep a clear focus, you'll produce a quality essay. Focus on content first, and then spelling and grammar. As long as your essay makes sense, you are on the right track. When you have a few minutes left, you can then go back and revise for spelling and grammar.

EXPOSITORY WRITING

Expository writing requires you to inform and explain a personal topic. Expository prompts are based on topics familiar to students and will ask you to describe or discuss the topic in detail and in a sequential order. You are able to draw on your own experiences and use background knowledge to develop your ideas for your composition or essay.

Aim to write four paragraphs that target the prompt's questions. You'll need a general opening paragraph, two body paragraphs that explain the questions, and a closing paragraph that wraps up your final thoughts. You don't want to give too much away in your introductory paragraph. Keep it general so that you can explain and expand your thoughts in the later paragraphs.

In this chapter, you will work through the steps of the writing process at a rapid pace. Try your best and focus on the content of your writing!

Pre-Writing / Planning Stage

Before you begin to write, map out the main ideas you'll be including in your writing. Since you'll want most of the 30 minutes to write and revise, you should not spend more than five minutes on your pre-write. Use bullet points, not full sentences, to make the most of your pre-writing time.

Given that you'll be writing four paragraphs, it would be a good idea to divide your paper into four sections, one for each paragraph. The top of each section should have your topic. For example, if you were writing about your favorite season, one of your topics could be "activities I enjoy during spring," with two bullet points that provide personal examples under that topic.

Your general paragraph can mirror the prompt. Often the prompt provides words that you can use in your essay writing. For example, if the prompt starts off with, "Seasons come and go, which is why we enjoy what each has to offer," you can use some of those ideas to get you started, and add a few personal touches as you go. Most importantly, you want to keep your writing clear, concise, and focused on a central theme.

Expository Prompts 1

Let's try **prewriting** for the following topics. Provide two bullet points (examples) for each topic.

1. What is your favorite hobby, activity, or sport, to participate in?

_____

_____

_____

_____

_____

_____

2. In what subject do you feel you excel in the most? Explain why.

_____

_____

_____

_____

_____

_____

_____

3. If you could travel anywhere in the world, where would it be, and why?

_____

_____

_____

_____

_____

_____

4. If you could meet any book character, who would it be? What qualities do you like the most in that character?

_____

_____

_____

_____

_____

_____

Expository Prompts 1: Possible Answers

1. **What is your favorite hobby, activity, or sport to participate in?**
   - Soccer is a sport I enjoy playing because I am part of a team.
   - I stay active and healthy.

2. **What subject do you feel you excel in the most? Explain why.**
   - Reading.
   - Books are a great way to learn and build a good vocabulary.

3. **If you could travel anywhere in the world, where would it be, and why?**
   - Italy would be a marvelous place to visit.
   - Visiting historical landmarks and eating the native food would help me learn more about the Italian culture.

4. **If you could meet any book character, who would it be? What qualities do you like the most in that character?**
   - Hank Zipzer.
   - He is funny, smart, and a typical fifth grade student. He always tries his best but finds troubles instead.

Your **pre-write** is essential in developing your expository essay. First, write an introduction paragraph that leads the reader to your topic. Then, begin to develop the points you've mapped out on your pre-writing sheet. As you start to develop your ideas, begin your body paragraphs. Here you will add details and examples that answer the questions in the writing prompt. Make sure your bullet points support your main idea. Finally, your last paragraph should be the conclusion of your essay. Wrap up what you've stated in your essay without repeating ideas. Instead, try to reflect on the memory, time, or instance you wrote about by adding in your emotions and feelings. Finally, good writers always revise and check their work. Leave yourself a little time to review what you've written and make last minute changes for spelling, punctuation, or grammar. Happy writing!

Expository Prompts 2

1. A friend is someone who is special to you. Friends make you laugh and you enjoy spending time with them. Write a composition about your best friend. What qualities do you like in that person? What are some things you enjoy doing together?

_____

_____

_____

_____

_____

_____

2. Dinnertime is a special time for a lot of families. It's a time when you can catch up about the day and share stories with the people you love. Write an essay about dinnertime in your house. What do you like most about it? Explain.

_____

_____

_____

_____

_____

3. School is a place where students come to learn and grow. Your teachers expect a lot from you and try to teach you in interesting ways. What is the most important thing you've learned in school? Write a composition that describes what you learned and why you think it's important for someone else to learn.

_____

_____

_____

_____

_____

_____

4. Vacation is a great time to relax with people you care about. What is the most memorable vacation you've taken? Who did you go with, and where? In a well-written composition, write about your vacation and what about it you liked most.

_____

_____

_____

_____

_____

_____

5. Teachers, parents, and friends are people who want the best for you. They want to see you learn, succeed, and grow. Write an essay about someone in your own life who has inspired you to do something that you enjoy, or encouraged you to take a challenge or risk. Explain how that person has been a positive influence or role model throughout this time in your life.

_____

_____

_____

_____

_____

_____

Expository Prompts 2: Possible responses

1. **A friend is someone who is special to you. Friends make you laugh and you enjoy spending time with them. Write a composition about your best friend. What qualities do you like in that person? What are some things you enjoy doing together?**

Best friends are special people in our lives. You can make friends anywhere, at anytime. There are many great friends in this world, but the best one you could ever ask for is already mine.

My best friend is Angie. We met in third grade at the beginning of the school year. We talked, played, and laughed, and soon became very close friends. We went over to each other's houses and went to birthday parties together. Angie is a great friend and a kind person.

"Do you like this bracelet?" Whenever Angie and I go shopping together, we always pick out clothes and accessories we think we'd both like. We love to share clothes! Angie is very stylish and enjoys dressing up. Angie is also very funny. She loves to tell jokes and have other people laugh. Her greatest talent is writing. She has a natural ability to tell fascinating stories with details and grace. Angelina has many qualities that I look for in a friend. I truly enjoy spending time with her.

The year is almost over and it's time to leave elementary school. I hope that Angie and I will continue to be friends when we enter middle school. I will always remember when Angie laughed so hard her face turned red. Also, the time she tripped over on the sidewalk and fell straight on her stomach. We laughed so hard we could barely breathe. We've shared many memories together. Angie is a spectacular friend, and I'm glad she's one of mine!

2. **Dinnertime is a special time for a lot of families. It's a time when you can catch up about the day and share funny stories with the people you love. Write an essay about dinnertime in your house. What do you like most about it? Explain.**

Dinnertime is a special time for a lot of families. It's a time when you can catch up about the day and share funny stories with the people you love. When parents leave for work and kids leave for school, they are later reunited at the dinner table.

"Let's eat! Who's hungry?" Most families look forward to dinnertime. The kitchen table is a great gathering place, especially in my family. We all enjoy getting together and sharing a conversation.

"Whose night is it?" my mom asks before heading to the grocery store. In my house, everyone is able to choose and plan a day for his or her favorite meal. We are responsible for planning the meal, preparing the food, and cleaning up afterwards. My sister's favorite meal is macaroni and cheese and chicken nuggets. My favorite dinnertime meal is Salisbury steak with string beans and mashed potatoes. It's a very well-rounded meal with meat, potatoes, and vegetables. Other nights, my dad requests hamburgers and hot dogs on the grill. Dinnertime is a very special time in my house because everyone has a say in what we eat.

"Who wants to talk about their day first?" my dad asks as we pass around the food for everyone to put on their plates. When we sit together, it's a time to reflect and share. A lot of times, my sister and I start talking about our day at school first. We then talk about the schedule of the events for the rest of the week. My dad always has a funny story about his day at work. He has a long commute into the city so he always tells us about what he sees on his way.

"Let's be thankful for what we have!" my mom always says at the end of the meal. Dinnertime reminds me and my family that we are very lucky to be able to sit down every night and share a meal. Oftentimes, we reflect on having enough food to eat and money to be able to live together. I hope that one day when I have my own family, I will be able to provide them with the stability and love that my parents provide me, especially at dinnertime. Dig in!

3. **School is a place where students come to learn and grow. Your teachers expect a lot from you and try to teach you in interesting ways. What is the most important thing you've learned in school? Write a composition that describes what you learned and why you think it's important for someone else to learn.**

School is a place where students come to learn and grow. Your teachers expect a lot from you and try to teach you in interesting ways. This is where some of the most important life lessons are learned and practiced.

"RRINNNGGGGGG!" When I entered fifth grade, I knew I'd be learning a lot of important things. The start of school always reminds me to be organized and to keep a clean desk. I learned that being organized is the key to success, and not just in school! Being organized will help you at home, with your friends, and even in your hobbies and activities. I knew that if I followed an organized path, I would have an extremely successful fifth grade year.

"You may now clean out your Language Arts section of your binder," my teacher says to us on Fridays. She always gives us a friendly reminder to clean out old work and tests. If you are not organized, you have the possibility of doing poorly on tests, quizzes and projects. You may also lose important notices that are supposed to go home to your parents. You don't want to be the only the student who doesn't get pizza on pizza days because you forgot the order form. "Pepperoni, please!"

I am elated with my performance as a fifth grade student. I followed all the rules and made a concerted effort to keep my binder, desk, and backpack clean and tidy. Through my newly learned organizational skills, I now keep a calendar in my bedroom to keep me aware of due dates. I also know when I'm able to play with friends after school. Being organized is the most important thing I've learned as a student. It is a life lesson that I will take with me everywhere I go.

4. **Vacation is a great time to relax with people you care about. What is the most memorable vacation you've taken? Who did you go with and where? In a well-written composition, write about your vacation and what you liked most about it.**

Vacation is a great time to relax with people you care about. Some vacation places are hot and humid, and some are cold and frosty. Others happen during your summer off from school, or over a holiday break.

"Kiwi! Kiwi!" I shouted as we passed a fruit stand. The most memorable vacation that I have ever been on was when I went to Myrtle Beach, South Carolina. I traveled there by car with my mom, dad, brother, and sister. It was such an exhilarating vacation. The warm weather, the cool breeze from the ocean, and delicious restaurants are some of the things that stand out to me on the best vacation ever.

"The Sun is blazing hot today. It's a scorching 101 degrees!" said the radio announcer. My family and I traveled to Myrtle Beach over our summer vacation. It was a wonderful time for us to be together and relax. My favorite part of the vacation was the pool and beach club. There, we played fun water games and ate lunch under a neon-green umbrella. Some days we played beach volleyball and collected seashells along the coast. We took plenty of photographs along the way. The most fascinating picture we took was an action shot of my brother diving for the volleyball. I can't wait to make a scrapbook documenting our adventures.

"New Jersey: 500 Miles," the sign read as we drove away from our resort. My family vacation was very enjoyable. I was glad I was able to spend the time playing and relaxing with my family. Next summer, I hope we go back to Myrtle Beach and swim with the dolphins. It would be a real thrill to be that close to one of my favorite animals. Every day I count down the days until summer vacation!

5. Teachers, parents, and friends are people who want the best for you. They want to see you learn, succeed, and grow. Write an essay about someone in your own life who has inspired you to do something that you enjoy or encouraged you to take a challenge or risk. Explain how that person has been a positive influence or role model throughout this time in your life.

Teachers, parents, and friends are people who want the best for you. They want to see you learn, succeed, and grow. Someone who inspires me to take a challenge or risk is my dad.

"GOOOOOOOOOOALLLLLL!" My dad is a huge inspiration to me. He is the person who first got me involved in soccer. He described all the rules of the game and even offered to help me practice. My dad was extremely patient and supportive. Put me in, coach!

"Practice makes perfect," is a saying my dad tells me to live by. My dad encourages me by coming to all of my games and providing me with positive feedback about my performance. He helps me maintain my strengths and work on my weaknesses. In addition, he takes me out for ice cream after every game, whether we win or lose. My dad is a great role model to learn from and I'm grateful to have a parent like him.

"It doesn't matter if you win or lose; it's how you play the game." That's one of my dad's favorite mantras. Although he enjoys when my team wins, he understands that it's just a game and we're still learning and practicing every day. He has also taught me a very important lesson in sportsmanship. I always make sure I'm polite and respectful, even if I'm feeling disappointed.

Everyone should have a positive influence in their lives. For me, my dad is that person. Not only with soccer, but he teaches me to work diligently and always do my best. I hope one day that I can be a positive influence on someone in my life. I love helping people. I would feel extremely proud of myself if I helped someone else find their passion, like my dad did with me and my soccer game.

Speculative Prompts

A **speculative prompt** poses a brief scenario that requires you to use your imagination to set up and finish the story. You may draw on a story you've read or from your own experiences to develop ideas for your composition.

Speculative prompts want you to use your imagination to solve a problem and come up with an appropriate solution for that problem. Although your imagination is required, you want to stick with what you already know. If you don't know anything about Egypt, you don't want the setting of your story to be there! Also, keep a clear focus on the story. Don't start off in Hawaii and end up in Africa. Stick to people, places, and situations you are familiar with to ensure that your story is clear and accurate.

As with any story, you'll need to add characters, a setting, a problem, and a solution. Make sure your story ends and isn't a cliff-hanger. Test scorers are looking for a completed story, not one that trails off. Here is a brief outline of how your essay should read:

Paragraph 1: Introduction

- Include a hook or grabbing topic sentence
- Onomonapeia, "boom!" "Crash!" "Chirp!" are great ways to get the reader's attention.
- Set up your story.

Paragraph 2: Body Paragraph

- Introduce your characters, setting, and problem.
- Address the character and the problem they are having.
- Provide examples and details.

Paragraph 3: Body Paragraph

- Begin to solve the problem presented in paragraph 2.
- Tie up loose ends and make sure all questions are answered.

Paragraph 4: Closing Paragraph

- Close your story.
- Allow your character some type of reflection; for example, "Ella knew that telling the teacher was the right thing and felt proud of herself for doing so."

Speculative Prompts 1

Try the following activity. Provide a **problem** and **solution** for each scenario.

1. Bailey sees that her friend is cheating on the science test by looking at the paper of the person sitting next to her.

   _____

   _____

   _____

   _____

   _____

   _____

2. Michael arrives at baseball practice and notices that his coach is missing but all the equipment has been set up.

   _____

   _____

   _____

   _____

   _____

   _____

3. Zaria shows up at school and has forgotten an important assignment.

_____

_____

_____

_____

_____

_____

4. Frankie is playing outside in his backyard when he notices something in the bushes.

_____

_____

_____

_____

_____

_____

Speculative Prompts 1: Possible Problems & Solutions

1. **Bailey sees that her friend is cheating on the science test by looking at the paper of the person sitting next to her.**

   Problem: Bailey is angry because she studied and her friend may get a better grade through cheating, which is wrong.

   Solution: Bailey tells the teacher who allows her friend to retake the test after she has studied at home.

2. **Michael arrives at baseball practice and notices that his coach is missing but all of the equipment has been set up.**

   Problem: They have a huge championship game and need their coach to review their plays and set up the batting order.

   Solution: They call the coach on a cell phone and learn that his car broke down on his way to get some snacks for the team. Parents offer to go and pick him up, and then they play ball!

3. **Zaria shows up at school and has forgotten an important assignment.**

   Problem: The biggest science project of the year is due and Zaria forgot to bring in the poster for the presentation.

   Solution: Zaria calls her sister who says she will bring it but Zaria will need to work on it during lunch.

4. **Frankie is playing outside in his backyard when he notices something in the bushes.**

   Problem: He's home alone and sees a big black bear.

   Solution: He remembers that his mom leaves a list of emergency numbers by the phone, so he calls Animal Rescue to take care of the bear and take him back to his normal habitat.

As stated before, **Speculative Writing** requires you to use your imagination to solve a problem or describe an adventure. Your essay should follow a similar format to the Expository essay. You will still need clear-cut paragraphs, transition words, and detailed sentences; however, in this essay, you'll need to present a problem and solve it by the end of your writing piece.

Speculative writing allows you to add dialogue, show conversation between characters, and describe the setting in which your story takes place. Remember, good writers develop their characters and give examples that show who they are and what they like to do. It's also important that you carefully read the prompt to identify any information that you should use in your writing. For example, the prompt may give you characters who have already been named, or a setting in which your story should take place. You'll want to make sure you mirror your writing after the information that is given.

Remember, if you have extra time, go back and check your writing. Be sure you have presented a problem and an appropriate solution by the end of your essay. Finally, proofread your writing for spelling and grammar. Good luck!

Speculative Prompts 2

1. The principal comes on the loudspeaker at lunch and announces that Jeremy and Todd need to meet him in the auditorium to discuss a very important matter. Write a story about Jeremy and Todd and what happens next.

_____

_____

_____

_____

_____

_____

_____

_____

_____

_____

_____

_____

_____

_____

_____

_____

_____

_____

_____

2. After school, Jenna patiently waits for her father to pick her up. When her dad arrives 20 minutes later, he explains that he has a big secret to tell her. Write a story about what the secret is and how it will affect Jenna.

_____

_____

_____

_____

_____

_____

_____

_____

_____

_____

_____

_____

_____

_____

_____

_____

_____

_____

_____

3. At the end of the day, Kayden walked home from school. When he arrived home, he saw a note left by his mother. She advised him she'd be home in an hour and to lock the door. Five minutes later, the doorbell rings. Write a story about Kayden, the person at the door, and what happens next.

_____

_____

_____

_____

_____

_____

_____

_____

_____

_____

_____

_____

_____

_____

_____

_____

_____

_____

_____

4. Maddie notices that the same girls disappear during recess to hang out in the bathroom. When Maddie walks in, she hears the other girls saying mean things about Olivia, Maddie's new best friend. Write a story about Maddie and how she deals with this problem.

_____

_____

_____

_____

_____

_____

_____

_____

_____

_____

_____

_____

_____

_____

_____

_____

_____

5. Jack planned an elaborate birthday party for himself and his closest friends. When the day of his party arrived, he realized that he had forgotten to pick up an important item for the party. Write a story about what you think he is missing, and what he does about it.

_____

_____

_____

_____

_____

_____

_____

_____

_____

_____

_____

_____

_____

_____

_____

_____

_____

_____

_____

Speculative Prompts 2: Possible Answers

1. The principal comes on the loudspeaker at lunch and announces that Jeremy and Todd need to meet him in the auditorium to discuss a very important matter. Write a story about Jeremy and Todd and what happens next.

McKinley is a fun and marvelous school, with the exception of Jeremy and Todd. These two boys were very kind, but they were always finding trouble. None of their teachers seemed to enjoy having them in class, until now.

"Jeremy! Todd! Come to the auditorium immediately," announced Mr. Ling, the principal. Jeremy and Todd were both at the same table and exchanged puzzled looks. Slowly, they got up and walked towards the auditorium. When they arrived, Mr. Ling was standing in the doorway, waiting. Todd and Jeremy were as scared as a deer getting chased by a hungry lion. Mr. Ling explained that an anonymous caller had blamed them for spray-painting the playground.

"We were framed! I swear!" screamed the boys in union. It was true. Todd and Jeremy did get in trouble a lot, but they never went looking for it. It was always detention for silly behavior, not for being disrespectful. Mr. Ling brought out the evidence; a bottle of spray-paint that had Jeremy's last name, Brown, written on the bottom. Mr. Ling figured that if Todd was involved with something, Jeremy wasn't far behind. The boys' punishment was suspension for a week.

The boys left the auditorium and headed home.

"Yeah, let's spray-paint it again tonight," whispered Tom, Todd's brother. Todd had overheard Tom's entire phone conversation. He couldn't believe that his brother was involved in such a disrespectful act.

"Hey, Tom!" Todd tried to say in a cool tone. "Is it true that you were involved in spray-painting prank?"

"Yeah, I did it! I spray-painted the whole jungle gym. Those kids won't be able to play on it for at least a month!" Tom bragged. "Don't say anything, or else I'll be in BIG trouble," he cautioned Todd.

Todd knew what he had to do. He rushed to the phone and called Mr. Ling and explained the situation. He told him that he knew it was his brother and that he and Jeremy really didn't have anything to do with the mess. The next day, the disaster was all sorted out and Todd and Jeremy were off the hook. They couldn't have been happier to be back in school.

"For once, we didn't do the wrong thing!" Todd said to Jeremy as they walked into woodshop.

2. **After school, Jenna patiently waits for her father to pick her up. When her dad arrives 20 minutes later, he explains that he has a big secret to tell her. Write a story about what the secret is and how it will affect Jenna.**

The hot days seemed to stand still. It was the last day of school and all Jenna wanted was to jump into her old pool and have a carefree summer. This didn't seem like a possibility because she was stranded at school. The bell had rung 20 minutes ago and her father still hadn't picked her up. She tried calling his cellphone, but only got his voice mail.

"You know you're twenty minutes late!" Jenna screamed at her father as he was smiling ear to ear. "What's your excuse this time, Dad?" she asked. She could tell that her father was itching to tell her something.

"Well, I have a secret to tell you," he said.

"A secret? What is it, Dad? Spit it out!" Jenna demanded.

"Our family is moving to Africa," her father announced.

"Africa! Africa? Where in the world did you come up with Africa?" Jenna asked. Jenna knew that since her mother had passed away, her father had a hard time maintaining their house. In a last-ditch effort, he decided it was the right time to sell the house and move to a new country. Jenna had imagined they'd move down the block or even across town, but not out of the country! A lot of emotions started running through her head, like meeting new friends and adjusting to a new school. Her father explained that they'd be staying with her mother's sister, Jean. "Oh, golly, I don't want to go there to spend time with Aunt Jean," Jenna whined.

Jenna didn't have anything against her aunt; it was just that she was the kind of aunt who'd pinch your cheeks every time she saw you. Plus, she painfully reminded Jenna of her mom. They were practically identical and had a lot of the same characteristics. Jenna's father told her it would be comforting to be around someone like her mother, which Jenna knew was true. That Saturday, they packed up the house, said their goodbyes, and were on their way halfway around the world.

Seventeen hours later they landed in Africa. They drove to Aunt Jean's and began to settle in. Jenna's father promised her that first thing the next morning they'd look for a house of their own to settle into. The next day, they found a small cottage on an animal reservation. It was fairly inexpensive and it was around animals, so they bought it on the spot. Jenna couldn't wait for peace and quiet and time alone with her father. The man who sold them their cottage reminded them that lions are often seen in the brush behind their house. Jenna got to thinking how nice it would be to have a whole bunch of animals living on their land.

"Bang!" heard Jenna from her bedroom. When she quickly ran outside, she saw what a hunter had done Jenna heard a small squeak from under a tree as the mother lion lay dead on the grass. Jenna recovered three cubs that were hiding from the hunter's gunfire. Their eyes were still crusted close and they were shaking from their scare. Jenna knew what they needed the most was a mother, just like she did. She knew that from now on, she'd raise the cubs like they were her own. Jenna now realized why they had moved in the first place. Her father wanted Jenna to build happy memories, away from the sadness of missing her mother.

Jenna and her father raised the cubs until they were strong enough to be on their own. They loved spending time with each other and enjoyed raising a new family together. Every day, Jenna hears their strong roars echoing in the forest.

3. At the end of the day, Kayden walked home from school. When he arrived home, he saw a note left by his mother. She advised him she'd be home in an hour and to lock the door. Five minutes later, the doorbell rang. Write a story about Kayden, the person at the door, and what happens next.

At the end of the day, Kayden walked home from school. When he arrived home, he saw a note left by his mother. She said she'd be back in an hour and to lock the door. But, as soon as the doorbell rang, however, he knew he'd forgotten to do what she asked.

"RINGGGG!" Running as fast as his legs could carry him, Kayden ran towards the front door, locked it, and slowly peered through the glass window. Before him stood a tall, slim man with dark hair and beady eyes. The man looked a bit ragged, wearing brown pants and a brown jacket. Kayden loosened the chain lock and opened the door a crack. "Who are you?" he asked.

The man seemed to open his mouth, as if talking, but instead of stating his name, he removed a piece of paper from his pocket. Kayden turned around and slammed the door, but when he did so, he had unlocked the chain and the door swung open.

"Hey, kid! This is a letter explaining I'm your new mailman," the man at the door tried to explain calmly. Before he knew it, Kayden had grabbed his baseball bat and was coming toward the man. When he got a closer look, he realized it was an official letter sent by the U.S. Postal Service. He felt terrible and apologized to the man, immediately.

"I'm so sorry, Mr. Mailman. It's just that I didn't know you and my mom always tells me not to let strangers in," he explained.

"I didn't mean to scare you, but I have a package here addressed for a Mr. Kayden Williams?." he said.

Kayden signed for it, and the mailman turned around and headed back to his truck. "See you tomorrow, Kayden!" the mailman yelled.

Fifteen minutes later, Kayden's mom arrived home. "Hi, Honey! How was your day?" she asked.

"It's great now that I have a package waiting for me to be opened!" Kayden said, enthusiastically.

"I told you not to answer the door, Kayden! It was supposed to be a surprise," she scolded.

Kayden thought that he did the right thing by signing for the package, but he assured his mom he would never open the door for a stranger again.

"Even if they had a million dollars?" his mother asked.

"Oh, come on, Mom! Don't tease me," Kayden joked.

From that day on, Kayden came home from school and locked the door immediately. He knew it was more important that his mother not worry about him, which was worth more than a million dollars to him.

4. **Maddie notices that the same girls disappear during recess to hang out in the bathroom. When Maddie walks in, she hears the other girls saying mean things about Olivia, Maddie's new best friend. Write a story about Maddie and how she deals with this problem.**

"She's stupid and mean," chattered the girls in the girls' bathroom. As Maddie walked in, she encountered Rachel and her friends talking badly about her friend, Olivia. Maddie often saw them sneaking into the bathroom during recess time. Now, she knew what they were up to.

"Ha! I left a note," Rachel bragged. "It said, 'Dear Olivia, you look like rust on a bicycle and smell like a rag! Love, Maddie!'" The other girls laughed in excitement as Rachel read the note she had made up. Just then, Maddie stepped up and confronted the mean girls.

"Hey, I didn't write that," Maddie defended. "You shouldn't talk about other people behind their backs. If you give that letter to Olivia, I'm going to tell Mrs. Hiddle," Maddie said.

"Let's go, girls. We're headed to the pool; and no, Maddie, you're NOT invited!" the girls said laughing, as they skipped away. Maddie was so angry. She couldn't believe those girls were acting so mean and were going to get away with it.

"I have to go tell Mrs. Hiddle," Maddie said to herself as she ran towards her classroom. As the bell rang, Maddie ran down the hall and found her teacher. She asked her and Olivia if they could talk outside.

"What's wrong, Maddie?" asked Olivia. She was such a sweet girl and truly cared if someone was upset.

"I heard some of the other girls saying mean things about you. I tried to defend you and they told me they were going to send you a mean note signed by me. I wanted you to know I'd never do that to you," Maddie explained.

"Who are the girls behind all of this?" Mrs. Hiddle asked. Maddie didn't want to tattle but knew it was the right thing to come clean and tell her the truth. She didn't care if the other girls liked her or Olivia. She would never regret doing the right thing.

Later that day, Mrs. Hiddle talked with Rachel and the other girls and had them write an apology letter to both Maddie and Olivia for their behavior. Maddie and Olivia knew that they'd never be friends with Rachel and the other girls, but both were happy they were taught a lesson. "I'm so glad we have each other," Maddie said to Olivia.

"Me, too! It's always better to be kind to everyone. I enjoy the friends I have because they'd never do anything mean to me," added Olivia.

5. **Jack planned an elaborate birthday party for himself and his closest friends. When the day of his party arrived, he realized that he had forgotten to pick up an important item for the party. Write a story about what you think he is missing, and what he does about it.**

"Jack, do you have everything ready for your birthday party in three days?" Jack's mom yelled to him upstairs. Jack carefully went over his list and told his mom he was all set. Many of his closest friends were coming to his party. He was so excited, it felt as if there were butterflies in his stomach.

On the day of the party, Jack realized an important item was missing. "Oh, Mom! I did forget something! The goodie bags!" Jack yelled down to his mother. As Jack was panicking, his mom tried her best to calm him down. "The party is tonight and we don't have any party favors to pass out!" Jack cried. Sulking in his room, he felt as if his party was ruined.

"YES!" shouted Jack. "I have an idea!" While Jack was running around, he began grabbing anything he could see to fit inside goodie bags. His mom grabbed some lunch bags and decorated them with each child's name. She also threw in a batch of her famous oatmeal raisin cookies in each bag. After hours of stressing, the goodie bags were finally assembled and complete. Jack felt relieved that his party was no longer ruined.

"Happy birthday to you!" Jack's friends sang as his mom brought out his big ice-cream cake. Jack's party turned out to be a great success. He was so proud of himself for planning fun games and activities, and even for assembling the goodie bags at the last minute. After cleaning up after the party, Jack sat down on the couch to rest. "What a great party!" he thought before he fell fast asleep.

REVISING AND CELEBRATING YOUR WRITTEN WORK

As you read in the introduction of this chapter, you only have a few minutes to revise and check over your work. This is not the time to change your entire essay completely; instead, you should be proofreading for spelling and grammar mistakes. The scorers know that it is a rough draft only, not a final copy. Start with major grammar and punctuation mistakes. If you are unsure of how to spell a word, try the best you can and circle it. That will tell the scorers that you attempted to use a word to make your story better, even though it may be spelled incorrectly.

Topic sentences and supporting details are two things that every good essay and story contains. Your topic sentences should tell the reader what your paragraph will be about. Remember: A new paragraph means a new idea. A quote, dialogue, or an overall synopsis about what the paragraph will be about is crucial to the structure of your essay. Supporting details can be specific instances, examples, or descriptions that answer the questions of the writing prompt.

Finally, be proud of the work you've written! It's a great accomplishment to be given a prompt without any preparation and to be able to write for thirty minutes. Any reader will realize you took the time to make a great first draft when you follow the structure provided in this chapter. Remember, too, to write as neatly as you can, keep a clear focus, and provide relevant details. If you have time, you can even give your story a title.

Good luck and happy writing!

Language Arts Literacy

Day 1

Section 1

You are now ready to begin Section 1 of Language Arts Literacy Practice Test 1. The test consists of reading passages and a writing task. The passages are followed by multiple-choice and open-ended questions.

If you finish early, check over your work. Remember, you may only check work in this section.

There are several important things to remember:

1. Read each passage carefully to learn what it is about. You may refer back to the reading passage as often as necessary.

2. Read each question carefully and think about the answer. Then choose or write the answer that you think is best.

3. When you are asked to write your answers, make sure to write them neatly and clearly on the lined pages provided at the end of this book.

4. For multiple-choice questions, make sure you fill in the corresponding circle in your answer folder.

5. If you finish a part of the test early, you may check over your work in that part of the test.

6. If you do not know the answer to a question, skip it and go on. You may return to it later, if you have time.

GO ON

105

Day 1
Section 1

You will have 30 minutes to complete the reading passages and the questions that follow. This section includes ten multiple-choice questions and one open-ended question. Work up to the page that has the "stop sign" on the bottom, or until time runs out.

If you finish early, check over your work. Remember, you may only check the work you've completed in this section.

Introduction: *To many, marine biologists are just whale watchers and dolphin trainers. This author explores and describes the various ways in which they help preserve our environment.*

Why Study Marine Biology?

Ever wonder what's underneath the ocean you swim in? Or how many fish survive in saltwater? If so, you're thinking like a marine biologist! Marine biologists not only study plant and animal life within saltwater habitats but they continue to research and develop ways to help maintain and preserve our environment.

The study of marine biology is a **rigorous** process. It includes the study of various sciences such as chemistry, microbiology, zoology, oceanography, and meteorology. Marine biology has helped the food cycle in many ways. Studying marine biology has helped scientists determine that marine life is an enormous resource that provides food and raw materials.

The scientific method plays an immense role when studying ocean and saltwater life. Marine biologists use their observations to make predictions, form hypotheses, and test their analyses through scientific experiments. Take bacteria, for instance. The ocean is full of bacteria, both beneficial and detrimental. Biologists are able to observe and examine bacteria to determine the process and flow of the food chain. Biologists are also able to identify new organisms that may hold the key to discovering new medicines and cures for health-related issues and diseases.

GO ON

Marine biology also requires the knowledge of environmental microbiology, which is the study of ocean health. Environmental biologists test and determine the quality of the water where organisms cohabitate. Biologists take a close look at pollutants, sediment, and coastal development in order to maintain a healthy and safe marine environment for people visiting or vacationing at the beach. Through the study of oil spills and chemical hazards, environmentalists help the outside world understand the long-term effects they have on our marine inhabitants.

Knowing that water covers at least 70% of our world, it's nearly impossible for scientists to explore all that marine life has to offer; however, marine biologists dedicate their careers to continuously surveying our environment. A healthy marine environment helps support life on the planet that we live on; therefore, it's important to understand why scientists study every aspect of the deep blue sea. For example, a change in climate is a simple notion that you've learned in school, but did you know that just a small change in climate affects the lives of many organisms in a marine environment? Every day scientists and environmentalists are studying ways to stop overfishing and the depletion of endangered species. In addition to studying organisms, research and development has since helped scientists discover alternate energy sources and prevent air quality from being compromised.

Although we are all not able to work as marine biologists, there are things that we can do to preserve and appreciate our marine environments. Get out there and see for yourself! We all have a little scientist in us who wants to observe, discover, and experience the wonder of living creatures and their living space. If you truly are interested in marine biology, ask your teachers to assign projects with live creatures or to point you in the direction of your local marine laboratory. Now, more than ever, organizations are offering programs that teach our youth how to conduct field science research and help protect threatened species and habitats.

When you're at the beach, take a look around. Experience all that our oceans and saltwater habitats have to offer. Next time you're swimming and your feet are digging into the ocean, you'll remember that you're standing above an entire world that we are continuing to explore.

GO ON

1. The writer begins with a question to
   A. create suspense about underwater life.
   B. interest the reader in marine biology.
   C. demonstrate the complexity of biology.
   D. inform the reader of dangerous environmental conditions.

2. In paragraph 2, the word **rigorous** means
   A. exciting.
   B. interesting.
   C. demanding.
   D. easy.

3. With which of these opinions does the writer of the article MOST LIKELY agree?
   A. Plant life is more important than animal life.
   B. You do not need to enjoy science to study marine biology.
   C. There are not enough supplies to study underwater life.
   D. Marine biology requires extensive knowledge of several science practices.

4. Why is it important for scientists to follow the scientific method?
   A. because they want to study ocean life
   B. because they need guidelines with which to work

   C. because they use their observations and predictions to perform experiments that help preserve our planet
   D. because it makes their jobs easier

5. What is the main idea of this article?
   A. Everyone should study to become a marine biologist.
   B. Marine biologists study more than just organisms and plants within a saltwater environment.
   C. Pollution is hurting marine plant life.
   D. Oil spills are dangerous to the sea animals.

6. In paragraph 4, environmental biologists are scientists who
   A. study oceans.
   B. examine tiny cells.
   C. only work with plants.
   D. only study animals.

GO ON

7. Scientists are unable to study all the ocean and saltwater environments in the world because
   A. they are happy with the research they've already collected.
   B. they feel it's unnecessary to investigate different environments.
   C. water covers 70% of the Earth, making it impossible to discover all marine environments.
   D. they do not have the equipment to observe other habitats.

8. This article would be most helpful for a student
   A. writing a paper on global warming.
   B. learning about meteorology.
   C. studying for a test on whales and dolphins.
   D. preparing a presentation on preserving our ocean and saltwater environment.

9. Studying oil spills allows scientists to
   A. predict long–term effects on the ocean's floor.
   B. clean up the mess.
   C. identify where the spill came from.
   D. see what organisms are affected by the spill.

10. Which one of these questions might a reader have after reading this article?
    A. Why is pollution so harmful to a marine environment?
    B. Why are oil spills harmful to saltwater habitats?
    C. How many endangered species are there in a marine environment?
    D. What other types of scientists play an important role in supporting and preserving marine life?

11. Open-Ended Question

As the article explains, marine biologists help protect threatened species and habitats through research and observation.

   • Explain one way marine biologists use observation to make scientific discoveries.

   • In your opinion, why is it important that we continue to study marine biology?

Use specific information from the story and any additional insight to support your response.

Write your response on the lined pages at the end of this book.

DO NOT GO ON
UNTIL YOU ARE
TOLD TO DO SO.

Day 1
Section 2

The following section requires you to write a response to an expository prompt. You will have 30 minutes to complete this part of the test. A space has been provided for you to use for prewriting and organizing your thoughts. Remember, nothing on your pre-write page will be scored.

Use the lined pages provided to write your response to the prompt's questions. When you are finished writing, be sure to check over your work in this section only.

Once the 30 minutes are over, put your pencil down and close your book.

Writing Task

If you could live the life of any animal for a day, what animal would you choose?

Write a composition that explains what you think would be the easiest and most difficult part about taking on the life of this animal. Support your answer with details and examples.

GO ON

Prewriting & Planning

_____

_____

_____

_____

_____

_____

_____

_____

_____

_____

_____

_____

_____

_____

_____

GO ON

Your Response

_____

_____

_____

_____

_____

_____

_____

_____

_____

_____

_____

_____

_____

_____

_____

_____

DO NOT GO ON
UNTIL YOU ARE
TOLD TO DO SO.

Day 1
Section 3

Directions: You will have 30 minutes to complete the reading passage and the questions that follow. This section includes 10 multiple-choice questions and 1 open-ended question. Work up to the page that has the "STOP" sign at the bottom, or until time runs out.

If you finish early, check over your work. Remember, you may only check the work you've completed in this section.

Introduction: *Freelance photography is the newest trend in modern technology. In this article, the author describes ways in which ordinary moments become lasting memories.*

GO ON

Fun With Photography

Imagine waking up every morning and walking into your living room instead of travelling to an office. Imagine only using the ideas you've thought up to plan your next adventure. Imagine being your own boss. Freelance photography allows all that and more.

Kate Nease, a self-employed, photographer, wants to accomplish one thing through her photos; to capture a memory. For Kate, it's not about the money or the credibility. Instead, creativity, technical expertise, and a "good eye" are essential in building Kate's successful enterprise. Kate uses her artistic vision to capture candid moments as they happen while using nature as her background.

When Kate first began her career as a freelance photographer, she was strolling through a New York City park at the beginning of spring. On her walk she noticed an encounter among several deer. Not wanting to scare them away, Kate took out her long lens and quietly began documenting the sweet, gentle demeanor of a mother and her offspring grazing in the grass. That moment was captured forever by just a simple point, click, and shoot.

On the other hand, taking candid photographs sometimes requires more than just quick thinking to create a unique image. "I've waited in all types of weather for an event or moment to happen. Sometimes, you're shown that perfect angle after a rainstorm or the breaking of dawn. I'm willing to wait for that split second of beauty because I know it's out there," Kate explains. Freelance photography allows for a greater sense of autonomy, artistic vision and, most importantly, self-expression. Through Kate's photos, she is able to tell a story through a series of individual images. Those images include all living creatures interacting naturally without preparation or planning.

Like many other passionate photographers, Kate Nease has also turned toward the modern age of digital cameras over traditional film cameras. Digital technology enables photographers to record images electronically. By uploading images instantly, she bypasses the old-fashioned way of sending film to a lab for processing. "Customers are looking for instant gratification. They want to see everything individually. I try and take pictures that remind people to enjoy the simple moments and group the pictures to tell the story," Kate further explains.

GO ON

114

Using nature as her background, Kate's **vocation** can happen anytime, anywhere. A sleeping dog, a bird's nest, or a single snowflake are all examples of recording beauty in nature. "I'm constantly being asked to shoot things like weddings, engagements, and birthday parties, but that's not me. I'm unconventional, independent, and completely focused on collecting images that are untouched," Kate says.

Kate's adventures have been funny (e.g., being chased down the street by a pigeon); rewarding (traveling to sacred places all around the world); and they've been tedious (waiting out a thunderstorm to capture raindrops on a rhododendron). "All in all, nature gives us so much. I'm just lucky enough to create lasting memories for others and be able to show my passion through my photos," Kate remarks.

Kate's story is a reminder that you can't plan a memory, it just happens. And if you're lucky, you'll be there to capture it.

GO ON

1. Which statement best summarizes the information given about Kate Nease's job?

    A. It pays her very well.

    B. She enjoys working in a studio.

    C. Her job makes her famous.

    D. Her main goal is capturing ordinary moments and making them lasting memories.

2. According to the article, how does Kate use "nature as her background"?

    A. She observes moments in nature as they happen, without planning.

    B. She sets up colorful backgrounds outdoors.

    C. She experiments with different lighting in her studio.

    D. She likes taking walks through parks.

3. Why does the author use the term, "point, click, and shoot"? at the end of paragraph 3?

    A. to suggest it's a hard skill to learn

    B. to indicate she doesn't take her job seriously

    C. to highlight the importance of technique

    D. to show that quick thinking often captures simple occurrences

4. Based on information from the article, why are more photographers turning to digital technology?

    A. They started to run out of film.

    B. It's easier to record images electronically and upload and view them instantly.

    C. It is difficult to find labs to develop film.

    D. Only digital cameras capture images clearly.

5. Which title BEST summarizes the information presented in the article?

    A. "1, 2, 3, Smile!"

    B. "Modern Technology Takes Over"

    C. "Making Memories Through Everyday Moments"

    D. "Wealth of Freelance Photographers"

6. What is Kate Nease's reasoning for not shooting weddings, engagements, or birthday parties?

    A. She's too busy.

    B. The editing process is too tedious.

    C. She enjoys taking unconventional photos.

    D. She doesn't like being around people.

GO ON

7. Using what you know from the story, which photo would Kate MOST LIKELY be interested in documenting?

   A. snow-covered tree branches

   B. a class photo

   C. celebrities at a movie premiere

   D. three dogs posing on a park bench

8. What does the word **vocation** mean in paragraph 6?

   A. career

   B. talent

   C. burden

   D. activity

9. What is the author's purpose in writing this article?

   A. to explain digital photography

   B. to highlight one of the many specialty areas within freelance photography

   C. to inform readers about how film is developed

   D. to entertain readers through nature

10. What happened as a result of Kate not interrupting the deer as they grazed?

    A. She walked through the park.

    B. The deer stopped eating because Kate got too close.

    C. Kate decided the background wasn't pretty enough.

    D. She was able to photograph the family of deer in their natural state.

11. Open-Ended Question

In this article, the author describes ways in which ordinary moments become lasting memories.

   • Describe one "ordinary" moment that freelance photographer Kate Nease captured.

   • If you were a freelance photographer, what scene would you be most interested in photographing? Explain your reasoning.

Support your answers with important details from the article.

Write your response on the lined pages at the end of this book.

STOP

DO NOT GO ON
UNTIL YOU ARE
TOLD TO DO SO.

Day 2
Section 1

You will have 30 minutes to complete the reading passage and the questions that follow. This section includes 10 multiple-choice questions and 1 open-ended question. Work up to the page that has the "STOP" sign on the bottom, or until time runs out.

If you finish early, check over your work. Remember, you may only check the work you've completed in this section.

Adventures in Cabin Cove

Juan and Lolita were always looking for their next adventure. The town pool, local park, and school playground had all been explored before. Juan knew that if he wanted to have an adventure he'd never forget, he'd need to recruit a partner in crime.

It didn't take much convincing to get Lolita on board. In fact, it was his sister Lolita's suggestion that led her and Juan to Cabin Cove. Cabin Cove was once a bright and cheery place. The air smelled of freshly cut wood and birds chirped in the distance. People often walked or hiked through the campsite to check on its condition. Cabin Cove's campground had recently been destroyed by a strong tornado. Although renovation plans were underway, the town was struggling to raise the rest of the money needed to restore it to the beautiful place it once was.

Lolita and Juan rode their bikes over the dirt path and through the vine-filled forest. Juan took the lead since he biked the path several times before; however, he was not expecting what he saw next. In front of him and Lolita was a blue-stone walkway that ran between rows of cabins. Once their bikes were parked, Juan and Lolita raced down the path. After walking for several minutes, they noticed a ruby-red cabin set slightly off the path they followed. "Juan, I've found our next adventure!" Lolita yelled as she zoomed ahead.

GO ON

Juan was reluctant to follow Lolita as she climbed the brick steps that led to the front door. "We shouldn't go in there, Lolita. We aren't even sure it's safe," pleaded Juan. Ignoring Juan's advice, Lolita grabbed his hand and unlocked the cabin door. They couldn't believe what they had just walked into. The inside of the cabin shined like a sparkling diamond. The walls were covered in framed mirrors and shelves that held glass potions and concoctions. A once reluctant Juan was now quickly perusing the wall for a potion to test. "Lolita, come check this out! It smells like licorice!" Juan exclaimed. As he was unscrewing the top to the turquoise vial, an old man appeared in the doorway of the cabin.

"My name is Monty. I am an energy healer. You have been led here to make an **imperative** decision. Choose wisely, young ones. These potions are powerful and will affect everyone. I will return once you have agreed on a cause," he stated.

Before Lolita and Juan could ask Monty any questions, he was gone. Juan paced the cabin as Lolita thoroughly examined the potions. "Juan, this potion says it can make us fly, and the orange one promises a wealthy life!" Lolita yelled out. "Wow, and this one says we can see the future!" she said excitedly. Although they both thought about using the potions for themselves, Juan realized what potion they truly needed to find.

"Check out this black bottle. It says it has the power to restore beauty to a place of our choice. I think this is why we were brought here," Juan reminded Lolita. "Imagine all the people who could benefit from a newly renovated Cabin Cove," he added.

"Juan, you're a genius! I feel silly for even suggesting that we use the potion for ourselves," Lolita said shamefully. At that moment, Monty appeared in a sleek, black cloak with a gold rope belt. He spoke harmoniously as he explained the terms in which the potion could be used.

"You may not tell anyone you were involved in this transformation. If you reveal that you were involved, the gift will be taken away. Last but not least, go straight home and do not look back. You cannot witness my magic. You have done a good deed. Be proud," Monty declared.

GO ON

Just then, Monty split the black bottle into two vials and directed Lolita and Juan out the cabin door and back down the blue-stone path. As they sprinkled the antidote across the campground, Juan and Lolita felt a great sense of pride knowing that they had a part in making Cabin Cove the place it once was.

After the last drop of potion was scattered, Juan and Lolita hopped on their bikes to head home. Monty appeared one more time and congratulated both of them on picking a worthy cause. Once again, before they could speak, Monty disappeared into the foggy air that now surrounded Cabin Cove. Just then, the wind picked up and the leaves rustled, but Lolita and Juan didn't look back as they continued towards home.

The next morning, Lolita and Juan's mom called upstairs to them, "Breakfast! Come down, you two, I want to show you something!" In her hands was the morning newspaper. The first page headline read, "Local Miracle Happens Overnight." Juan and Lolita gazed at the picture that took up the entire page. There it was: Cabin Cove completely transformed. Each cabin was painted a vibrant color and the blue stone path they walked just yesterday outlined a once decadent courtyard now filled with exotic plants and flowers. "The paper claims that a man who calls himself 'M' is somehow responsible for the makeover overnight," their mom read.

"How do they know that?" questioned Lolita.

"A note was tacked to one of the cabins. A red cabin, actually," she continued on.

"And what did it say, Mom?" asked Juan.

"It said, 'Those who contribute selflessly experience true fulfillment,'" she answered. "Sounds very philosophical."

"M sounds more like an energy healer," Juan remarked.

"What is an energy healer?" their mom asked.

Juan and Lolita turned to each other and smirked. That day turned out to be more than just an adventure. It was an experience of a lifetime that gave them an opportunity to make a difference.

GO ON

1. Which one of the following adjectives best describes both Juan and Lolita?
   A. relaxed
   B. casual
   C. dreary
   D. thrill seeking

2. In paragraph 4, the sentence, "The inside of the cabin shined like a sparkling diamond," is an example of
   A. imagery.
   B. a metaphor.
   C. a simile.
   D. personification.

3. Which of the following describes how Cabin Cove's campground was destroyed?
   A. a hurricane
   B. a tornado
   C. a tsunami
   D. an earthquake

4. In the fifth paragraph, the word **imperative** can be replaced by which of the following?
   A. important
   B. minor
   C. small
   D. exciting

5. What is the overall message of this story?
   A. People who are adventurous have the most fun.
   B. Treat your best friend with respect.
   C. Always put yourself first.
   D. Perform acts that help others and make a difference.

6. All of the following are potions that Lolita suggested EXCEPT
   A. a potion that guarantees straight A grades.
   B. a potion that allows you to fly.
   C. a potion that tells the future.
   D. a potion that promises a wealthy life.

7. In paragraph 11, the sentence, "Just then, the wind picked up and the leaves rustled, but Lolita and Juan didn't look back as they continued towards home," implies that
   A. Lolita and Juan were scared.
   B. Monty was beginning to perform his magic.
   C. an animal was hiding in the bushes.
   D. Lolita and Juan's mom was following them.

GO ON

121

8. According to the passage, why were the renovations of Cabin Cove incomplete?

   A. Towns people didn't want a new campsite.

   B. All the workers were on vacation.

   C. The town was struggling to raise the money needed to finish the project.

   D. People forgot the campsite had been destroyed.

9. This passage was MOST LIKELY written to

   A. persuade adults to donate to local causes.

   B. entertain readers through adventure and discovery.

   C. inform readers of the danger of tornados.

   D. explain Lolita and Juan's relationship.

10. Monty left a note on the door of the ruby-red cabin because

   A. that was the cabin where Lolita and Juan found the potions.

   B. red was his favorite color.

   C. it was the closest cabin to the walkway.

   D. he wanted Lolita and Juan to remember him.

11. Open-Ended Question

Juan and Lolita were looking for an adventure and found a potion that would restore beauty to any place.

- Imagine that Juan and Lolita never selected the potion that Monty used. Describe another potion they could have agreed on to help fix Cabin Cove.

- In your opinion, who was more adventurous, Juan or Lolita? Why? Support your answer with details from the story.

Write your response on the lined pages at the end of this book.

CLOSE YOUR
TEST BOOKLET

Day 2

Section 2

The following section requires you to write a response to a speculative prompt. You will have 30 minutes to complete this part of the test. A space has been provided for you to use for prewriting and planning your thoughts. Remember, nothing on your prewrite page will be scored.

Use the lined pages provided to write your response to the prompt's questions. When you are finished writing, be sure to check over your work in this section only.

Once the 30 minutes is over, put your pencil down and close your book.

Writing Task

Hannah and Lucy couldn't wait for summer vacation. As they stepped onto the beach, Lucy spotted a huge sign by the lifeguard stand and realized they were facing a huge dilemma.

Write a story about Lucy and Hannah's dilemma. Explain the problem they were facing and how they solved it.

GO ON

123

Prewriting and Planning Space

GO ON

Your Response

_____

_____

_____

_____

_____

_____

_____

_____

_____

_____

_____

_____

_____

_____

CLOSE YOUR
TEST BOOKLET

Language Arts Literacy

Day 1

Section 1

You are now ready to begin Section 1 of Language Arts Literacy Practice Test 2. The test consists of reading passages and a writing task. The passages are followed by multiple-choice and open-ended questions.

If you finish early, check over your work. Remember, you may only check work in this section.

There are several important things to remember:

1. Read each passage carefully to learn what it is about. You may refer back to the reading passage as often as necessary.

2. Read each question carefully and think about the answer. Then choose or write the answer that you think is best.

3. When you are asked to write your answers, make sure to write them neatly and clearly on the lines provided in your answer folder.

4. For multiple-choice questions, make sure you fill in the corresponding circle in your answer folder.

5. If you finish a part of the test early, you may check over your work in that part of the test.

6. If you do not know the answer to a question, skip it and go on. You may return to it later if you have time.

GO ON

Day 1
Section 1

You will have 30 minutes to complete the reading passages and the questions that follow. This section includes 10 multiple-choice questions and 1 open-ended response. Work up to the page that has the "stop sign" on the bottom, or until time runs out.

If you finish early, check over your work. Remember, you may only check the work you've completed in this section.

A Lesson Learned

"Be ready to discuss Chapters 2 and 3 on Wednesday," Mrs. Herbert announced as the bell signaled the end of class. Students shuffled out of the classroom and proceeded down the crowded hallway to the cafeteria. Lisa and Jess waited by the stairway for the rest of their friends, while glancing over at the group of boys across from them.

"Caught you!" Amy's voice shouted, completely startling Jess and Lisa, while they were shyly looking over to where the boys were standing.

It was no secret that Jess had a crush on Mark, the tall, dark-eyed, curly-haired athlete who captured the attention of many of the 6th grade girls. The group of friends whispered and giggled all the way to the cafeteria, then proceeded to their table—the one that didn't officially have their names on it but might as well have since no one else would even think of sitting there.

Lunch period was a mixture of loud voices, smells of pizza and sandwiches, students scurrying to chat with friends, and the occasional aluminum foil ball flying towards its intended target. The girls were discussing Lisa's awesome haircut, Amy's new boots, the twins' overprotective mom, and Mark, who was sitting two tables down from them. It was a typical lunch period for Jess and her friends.

A completely different scene was occurring a few feet away, at the table right next to Jess and her crew—nine seats, all empty, with the tenth one occupied by a girl

GO ON

slowly nibbling at her sandwich. She didn't look anything like the others, this strange student with her bright orange hair cropped much too short, her out-of-style clothing (which was too large for her small frame and seemed to be hanging off her body) and her odd-looking eyes, which were just a slight bit too large for her face. It was difficult not to notice her, although her expression at that moment seemed to say that was exactly what she was hoping for: to stay unnoticed.

"Ughh," Lisa groaned in disgust as she glanced at the girl sitting alone at the table. "I can't take another day of looking at her while I'm eating!"

"Why can't she just go eat in the library or something?" Amy chimed in. "I mean, she knows everyone in here is talking about her. Why would she even want to be here?"

Jess nodded in agreement. "She deserves what she gets. What a weirdo! She doesn't even attempt to look or act normal! She's a real freak! Hey…Freaky Fran! What a perfect name!"

Everyone at the table began laughing, and in a few moments, taunts of "Freaky Fran! Freaky Fran!" were heard coming from the group of girls and echoing throughout the cafeteria. Like wildfires in a dry forest, the chant spread from one end of the room to the other as students stood up, faced the red-faced girl who seemed to be shrinking further into her oversized clothing, and began bellowing, "Freaky Fran! Freaky Fran!"

Sara, one of the twins, watched as the scene unfolded. A strange, unpleasant feeling came over her; an uncomfortable feeling she couldn't quite describe. Her head was telling her, "Make it stop. This is wrong." Yet, her mouth would not allow her to utter these words, and she felt sad, confused, and helpless as she sat and witnessed behavior she knew she should stop. Quietly, she slid out of her seat and slipped out of the cafeteria, unnoticed by her friends.

As the teachers and lunch aides caught on to what was happening, the girls effortlessly shifted their conversation to Friday night's football game. They had had their fun and were finished with their little game.

As the final bell of the day rang, students emptied out of the building, joining their groups of friends as they headed home. Sara told her friends that she needed to get some work done in the library, so the rest of the group left for home without her.

GO ON

Sara's legs felt like weights as she dragged them up the three flights of stairs to the library. She knew she would find Fran there. She was always there. Standing outside the door for what seemed like an eternity, Sara finally found the courage to walk in and in no time at all, her eyes spotted Fran working diligently at the table in the right-hand corner of the room. Sara forced herself to approach her. Fran was startled by the girl standing next to her, and her face turned a crimson color as if it were burning. The next few moments were quite **awkward**, with no words spoken between the two girls. Finally, the deafening silence was broken by, "My name is Sara." Silence. Sara fidgeted and looked at the floor while she nervously uttered, "I'm sorry for what happened today."

Again, a silence that seemed to last forever. Sara waited for a reply, but when none came, she finally looked up, and much to her surprise, found Fran staring right at her with a sad but strong look in her eyes.

"Why couldn't you look at me when you said that?" asked Fran in a matter-of-fact tone. "Am I that repulsive that you can't even look at me when you talk to me?"

Sara was stung by the question. She never expected such a response, especially after apologizing for something she really didn't even take part in! Much to her surprise, Sara could not find the strength inside of her to face Fran, but instead, continued to stare blankly at the floor, embarrassed by her own reaction. "Why can't I look at her?" she asked herself over and over again.

"Humiliation is something I deal with every day of my life," Fran whispered. "I've lived with it for so long that you would think I would be used to it by now. But guess what? I'm not. Every time I hear words like I heard today, sit alone at a table, feel the stares and snickers coming from all directions, it hurts. It hurts so bad you could never imagine it. I ask myself every day, 'What's wrong with me? What have I said or done to make everyone hate me so much?' I come to school with a sick feeling in the pit of my stomach every morning and cry myself to sleep every night. That's my life. That's what 'normal' is for me."

Sara did not know what to do or say. She seemed frozen, a block of ice standing next to Fran, unable to look up from the wooden floor. Out of nowhere, Fran gently touched Sara's chin and slowly lifted her head so they were staring directly into one

GO ON

another's eyes. They stayed that way for a few seconds, but it seemed so much longer to Sara, who started to get that sick feeling inside of her again. Fran spoke so softly, her words were like a soft breeze that brushes your face for an instant and then disappears. "I will be here after school tomorrow. If you have something you would like to say, I'll listen. But I need you to do something for me. Look at me when you say it. See me. I'm right here. All I've ever wanted was for people to realize that I am a person, too. Just like them. Look in my eyes when you talk to me. That's all I ask."

Fran packed up her books, took one last look at Sara, and walked away. Sara's eyes filled with tears as she found herself once again staring down at the floor.

GO ON

1. Which of the following best describes the group of girls in the story?

   A. very close friends and totally loyal to one another

   B. extremely popular and admired by most of the students in the school

   C. active and involved in a variety of school activities

   D. a group who believes they are better than most of their peers and can do as they please

2. What is the most likely reason that Fran wanted to "stay unnoticed" while she was eating her lunch?

   A. She was embarrassed by the way she looked.

   B. If people didn't notice her, she might avoid getting teased and made fun of.

   C. She would rather eat lunch by herself than with others.

   D. She was very shy and did not like to attract attention to herself.

3. Which quote from the passage leads you to believe that the girls felt they had a right to make fun of Fran?

   A. "She doesn't even attempt to look or act normal!"

   B. "I mean, she knows everyone in here is talking about her."

   C. "I can't take another day of looking at her while I'm eating!"

   D. "She's a real freak! Hey…Freaky Fran! What a perfect name!"

4. Sara knew that the teasing was wrong, but did not put a stop to it. What was most likely the reason for this?

   A. She wasn't taking part in the teasing, so it really was none of her business.

   B. She was afraid of the reaction she would get from her friends if she did speak up.

   C. She thought that by speaking up, the others might pick on Fran even more.

   D. She didn't believe she had the right to get involved.

5. What literary device is used in paragraph 13 when the author states, "Finally, the deafening silence was broken…"

   A. metaphor

   B. oxymoron

   C. personification

   D. hyperbole

GO ON

6. As Sara walked up to the library, her legs "felt like weights as she dragged them up the three flights of stairs…" (paragraph 13). What is the author trying to say to the reader?

   A. Sara is dreading what she is about to do.

   B. Climbing three flights of stairs is very tiring and made her legs feel like heavy weights.

   C. Sara is feeling forced to apologize to Fran, and she doesn't really want to.

   D. Sara is walking slowly to keep a lookout for any of her friends, as she does not want them to discover she is looking for Fran.

7. Which of the following would be the best theme for this selection?

   A. Love and Friendship

   B. Revenge

   C. The Power of Words

   D. Good vs. Evil

8. Why is it so important to Fran that Sara make eye contact when she speaks to her?

   A. She wants to see if Sara is being truthful.

   B. She is trying to develop a friendship with Sara.

   C. She views this as a sign of respect and recognition that all people deserve.

   D. If Sara looks at her when she speaks, Fran might begin to believe that she is not so strange and unpopular.

9. From what you have learned about Sara, which is the best prediction of what she will do the next day?

   A. She is so ashamed of what she did that she will not attempt to meet Fran in the library.

   B. She will tell her friends what happened, and ask them all to apologize to Fran.

   C. She will write Fran a letter explaining that she really had nothing to do with the cafeteria incident.

   D. She will meet Fran alone in the library, look her in the eyes, and apologize again.

10. As it is used in paragraph 13, what is another word for **awkward**?

   A. stubborn

   B. uncomfortable

   C. clumsy

   D. bulky

GO ON

11. Open-Ended Question

Bullying occurs in schools everywhere and educational programs have been put into place to stop this horrible abuse.

- Would you consider the cafeteria incident in this passage to be a form of bullying? Why or why not?
- What might Sara have done differently when she first felt that strange, unpleasant feeling come over her?

Use specific information from the story and any additional insight to support your response.

Write your response on the lined pages at the end of this book.

DO NOT GO ON
UNTIL YOU ARE
TOLD TO DO SO.

Day 1
Section 2

The following section requires you to write a response to an expository prompt. You will have 30 minutes to complete this part of the test. A space has been provided for you to use for prewriting and organizing your thoughts. Remember, nothing on your pre-write page will be scored.

Use the lines provided to write your response to the prompt's questions. When you are finished writing, be sure to check over your work in this section only.

Once the 30 minutes are over, put your pencil down and close your book.

Writing Task

The principal of your school has just announced that she will be putting a new rule into effect beginning next week. All the students are upset by this sudden change. Write a story about the principal's new rule, why everyone is upset about it, and what happens next.

GO ON

Prewriting & Planning

_____

_____

_____

_____

_____

_____

_____

_____

_____

_____

_____

_____

_____

_____

_____

_____

GO ON

Your Response

DO NOT GO ON
UNTIL YOU ARE
TOLD TO DO SO.

Day 1
Section 3

You will have 30 minutes to complete the reading passage and the questions that follow. This section includes 10 multiple-choice questions and 1 open-ended question. Work up to the page that has the "STOP" sign at the bottom, or until time runs out.

If you finish early, check over your work. Remember, you may only check the work you've completed in this section.

Rain Forests at Risk

Growing industries are destroying Borneo's rain forest. Can the jungle and its animals be saved?

In the not-too-distant past, hundreds of thousands of orangutans could be found swinging through the jungles of Southeast Asia. Fast-forward to the present: There are fewer than 60,000 of the great apes left in the wild. Orangutans are listed as endangered. Development is putting them at an even greater risk. The rain forests of Indonesia and Malaysia are the last remaining habitats for the apes. But for how much longer?

The Vanishing Jungle

Borneo's rain forest is one of the most biologically diverse places on Earth. It is home to thousands of types of plants and hundreds of animal species. About 90% of all orangutans live on the island of Borneo, which is divided between Indonesia, Malaysia and Brunei. The rest live on the Indonesian island of Sumatra. Orangutans spend most of their lives climbing, eating, and sleeping in the forest canopy. They are the world's largest arboreal, or tree-dwelling mammals.

In the past three decades, deforestation has claimed nearly 80% of the apes' jungle home. As the forests disappear, so do the species that rely on them for survival.

GO ON

Humans suffer too. Rain forests play a role in reducing carbon dioxide (CO_2) gases that trap heat in the atmosphere. Without trees to absorb it, billions of tons of CO_2 stay in the air, which can speed up climate change.

Forestry expert Amity Doolittle says that illegal logging and the growth of the palm-oil industry are the main culprits of deforestation. Palm-oil companies cut down vast areas of jungle to build plantations. "The clearing is done on such a large scale that you feel as if you are in the desert," Doolittle says.

Defenders argue that the palm-oil industry creates jobs. A study by World Growth, a group that supports economic growth in poor nations, found that 20 million Indonesians earn a living through palm oil. The product can be found in everything from cookies to soap.

Save the Rain Forests!

Still, economic growth comes at a price. That is why consumers and environmental groups are demanding that companies make palm oil **sustainable** and that they set guidelines to protect forestland.

Biruté Mary Galdikas has been studying orangutans in Borneo for 40 years. Her work is featured in the film "Born to be Wild." She says the creatures have taught her humility. "The best thing you can do to help them is to be aware," she says. "Read product labels. Be responsible."

Fast Facts

Branch out and gain knowledge of these great apes!

– In the Malay language, orangutan means "person of the forest."

– Orangutans feed mainly on forest fruits such as durians, mangoes, and figs. They also eat leaves, insects, honey, bark and occasionally, small animals.

GO ON

– The resourceful apes sometimes use large leaves as shade from the sun and as umbrellas in the rain.

– Almost every night, orangutans build new nests made of branches to sleep in.

1. What is this story mainly about?

   A. What we must do to save the rain forests

   B. How deforestation in Borneo is threatening orangutans

   C. What Biruté Mary Galdikas is doing to help orangutans

   D. How orangutans are different from other great apes.

2. Forests in Borneo are being cleared away because of

   A. illegal logging.

   B. the growth of the palm oil industry.

   C. pollution.

   D. both A and B.

3. According to the article, palm oil companies are affecting Indonesia in ways that are:

   A. only good.

   B. only bad.

   C. both good and bad.

   D. none of the above.

4. Arboreal animals include all of the following **except**

   A. lions.

   B. parrots.

   C. koala bears.

   D. monkeys.

5. What is the author's purpose for making the following statement found in paragraph 6? "The product can be found in everything from cookies to soap."

   A. to help us realize it is our fault that rain forests are at risk

   B. to show the wide range of items that contain palm oil

   C. to convince us that we need palm oil in our everyday lives

   D. to discourage us from buying these items

6. In this passage, what is the meaning of **sustainable?**

   A. illegal in the rain forest

   B. usable

   C. much more expensive to purchase

   D. able to use without causing severe damage to nature

GO ON

7. In the **Fast Facts** section, the author describes the orangutans as being resourceful animals. Which is NOT an example of an animal showing how resourceful it is?

   A. Crows turn all types of objects into useful tools for getting food from hard-to-reach places.

   B. If a wolverine is slower than its prey, it will climb a rock or tall stump and jump on its prey, breaking vital organs in its body.

   C. Sea otters often keep a rock in a loose pocket of their skin to use when needed to break open shellfish and clams.

   D. Elephants may have offspring up until the approximate age of 50.

8. Why does Biruté Mary Galdikas suggest that we read product labels?

   A. So that we can be aware of products that contain palm oil and limit the number of these items that we purchase.

   B. So that we can buy products that help the Indonesian people keep their jobs.

   C. So that we make sure we do not buy any products containing palm oil.

   D. So we can find out where the product is made.

9. Why did the author most likely write this article?

   A. to create empathy for orangutans

   B. to inform the reader of the dangers rain forests are facing

   C. to persuade the reader to become more aware of our own actions, and to do what we can to help reduce the risks to rain forests

   D. to entertain us with fun facts about orangutans

10. When Amity Doolittle compares the cleared forests to a desert, what is she trying to convey to her readers?

   A. She wants her readers to picture the once lush, green forest as a barren, empty place.

   B. She is trying to persuade her readers to write letters to their senators about the hazards of deforestation.

   C. She is using exaggeration to get her readers to feel sympathetic to her cause.

   D. She knows that most people prefer rain forests to deserts.

GO ON

11. Open-Ended Question

Provide at least two detailed reasons why rain forests are at risk.

- Then explain their importance to humans and animals, citing examples from the passage.

Support your answers with important details from the article.

Write your response on the lined pages at the end of this book.

CLOSE YOUR
TEST BOOKLET

Day 2
Section 1

You will have 30 minutes to complete the reading passage and the questions that follow. This section includes 10 multiple-choice questions and 1 open-ended question. Work up to the page that has the "STOP" sign on the bottom, or until time runs out.

If you finish early, check over your work. Remember, you may only check the work you've completed in this section.

Introduction: *Stand in a park or on the beach on a windy day, and chances are that if you look up, you will see a kite flying in the air. This author explores the history of kite flying, and gives us some insight about the importance of kites around the world.*

Go Fly a Kite

A kite catches the wind. Tugging at the string, it pulls upward, dipping and swaying. The string unwinds. The kite climbs higher and higher into the blue. Its colorful shape looks beautiful against the sky. Flying a kite is a fun way to spend a spring day.

People around the world have been flying kites for centuries. In fact, kites were invented over two thousand years ago! One ancient story tells of a Chinese general named Han Hsin. He was in charge of a small army. The army was trying to overthrow a cruel emperor. Han Hsin built a kite and had his soldiers fly it in the direction of the palace. When the kite was over the palace, Han Hsin marked the string, then reeled in the kite.

Then he measured his string from the mark to the kite. He used this measurement to plan a tunnel to the palace. His soldiers crept through the tunnel, popping up inside the walls of the palace! The cruel emperor was defeated with the help of a simple kite!

GO ON

Kites have also been used in modern warfare. Before airplanes were invented, cameras were tied to kites. They were sent high in the air to take pictures. This was a way of gathering information about enemy forces.

Kites have also been used to carry radio equipment up in the air. This made the signals easier to send and receive. In World War II, kites were used as targets for shooting practice. Kites were also included as part of the emergency kits in lifeboats. People stranded in lifeboats could fly the kites. Searchers would see the kites and come to their rescue.

Kites have been used in many other ways as well. People have used kites to carry instruments high into the clouds. There, the instruments measured temperature and wind speed. Sometimes the kites could not fly high enough. When this happened, they were often tied together in trains. First, one kite was sent sailing on a long string. This string was tied to a second kite. This kite helped to lift the first kite even higher. A third and even a fourth kite might be added to the train.

One famous event involving a kite was Benjamin Franklin's experiment. Franklin wanted to show that lightning was a form of electricity, and he thought that if he sent a kite up into the clouds he could find out for sure. Franklin made his kite carefully. He used two lightweight sticks and covered them with a square of silk fabric. He attached an iron wire to the frame of the kite. Then he attached a long string. Near the end of this string, Franklin tied a brass key. Franklin then tied a piece of silk ribbon to the end of the string, which he would use to hold onto the kite.

On a stormy afternoon, Franklin set out to try his kite. A brisk breeze was blowing, which helped the kite rise quickly into the dark clouds. Raindrops were pelting down. As a safety measure, Franklin stood in the doorway of a barn. Water is a good conductor of electricity, and he knew he needed to keep the silk ribbon dry. Franklin reached out and tapped the key with his finger. Sparks flew! It was electricity!

Franklin was happy with the results of his experiment. He was also very lucky. It is very important to remember that you should never fly a kite on a stormy day. Metal should never be used in the making of kites. Also, kites should never be flown around power lines.

GO ON

Today, kites are used mostly for fun. Families go to open spaces like parks or beaches to fly kites. Sometimes there are even kite-flying contests.

In China, there is a special holiday called Kites' Day. There is a legend that is told on this day. The legend says that long, long ago a man in China dreamed that his house and family would be destroyed on the ninth day of the ninth month. On that day, he took his family up into the hills. Together, they flew kites all day. When they returned home, they found their house had tumbled down, and there was nothing left but a pile of rubble. But the family was safe.

Now, on the ninth day of the ninth month, many Chinese people go outside and fly kites. The kites are made to look like brightly colored birds, graceful butterflies, or even enormous dragons. The hopes is that the flying of the kites will bring good luck.

In Japan, special kites are flown on May 5. This holiday was first called Boys' Day. On this day, families would fly kites to celebrate the birth of baby boys during the past year. Each family also flew windsocks. Windsocks are a kind of kite. They were flown on a tall bamboo pole. There was a windsock for each boy in the family. Each windsock was shaped like a carp: a very strong fish. A carp can swim against a strong current and was a symbol of the hard work and courage needed to succeed in life. Today, girls are included in the celebration. The name of the holiday has been changed to Children's Day, and kites and windsocks are still part of the fun.

Kites can be large and elaborate, or small and simple. Many kites are very inexpensive. You can even make a kite of your own, using nothing more than sticks, paper, tape, and a ball of string. So, the next time you are looking for something fun to do, go fly a kite!

GO ON

147

1. The author most likely titled this story "Go Fly a Kite" because
   A. He thought that using an idiom for a title would add a bit of humor.
   B. He wanted to offer a suggestion for something to do when you are bored.
   C. He wanted to give the reader a clue that the story was about kites.
   D. The story teaches the reader how to make and fly kites.

2. What is most likely the author's purpose in telling the story of Han Hsin starting in paragraph 2?
   A. to give the reader an idea of how government was run in ancient China
   B. to explain the role of an emperor in ancient China
   C. to give the reader an example of a different use of a kite in the past
   D. to show the reader how old kites really are

3. What was the reason for tying kites together when measuring temperature and wind speed?
   A. To gather more information from a number of kites rather than just one.
   B. At times, a kite could not fly high enough to gather the information it needed.

   C. If kites were tied together, they would be more visible from the ground.
   D. Tying kites together made sure that the information obtained was accurate.

4. Why did Benjamin Franklin most likely tie a piece of silk ribbon to the end of the string?
   A. So it would be easier to hold the string during a strong storm
   B. Silk is not a good conductor of electricity and would keep him safe.
   C. Silk was the only fabric available in that time period.
   D. Silk came from China where kites first came from.

5. The author mainly used contrast in this article by
   A. showing the many different ways kites were used.
   B. discussing the changes made to Boys' Day in Japan.
   C. explaining the difference between how ancient kites and modern kites looked.
   D. showing the difference between the main uses of ancient kites compared to kites today.

GO ON

6. The author would most likely agree with which of these opinions?

   A. The use of kites on lifeboats is the most important of all the uses mentioned in the passage.

   B. Making kites is the best activity for children on a rainy day.

   C. Kites have had many important and interesting uses throughout history.

   D. Kites are more popular now than they were in ancient times.

7. This article would be MOST helpful to a student who

   A. wants to create a poster demonstrating the many different uses of kites around the world.

   B. wants to learn how to make a kite.

   C. needs to study for a test on the culture of China.

   D. needs to write a report about Children's Day.

8. What is the BEST summary of paragraph 13?

   A. The carp is a symbol of hard work and courage.

   B. Boys are held in high regard in the country of Japan.

   C. Windsocks and kites are very similar.

   D. May 5 is a special day for family kite-flying in Japan.

9. What can the reader infer by the author's statement that "Franklin was also very lucky"?

   A. He believed Franklin's experiment would make him famous.

   B. He meant that he was lucky the weather turned out the way it did so the experiment was a success.

   C. He believed that Franklin could have been badly injured or even killed.

   D. He realized what Franklin's discovery meant to the world.

10. What type of literary element does the author use in paragraph 1?

    A. hyperbole

    B. personification

    C. simile

    D. metaphor

GO ON

11. Open-Ended Response

This passage introduces the reader to the many uses of kites over the years in all parts of the world.

- Discuss two uses of kites as mentioned in the story. How were these uses important? Support your answer with details from the article.

Write your response on the lined pages at the end of this book.

CLOSE YOUR
TEST BOOKLET

Day 2

Section 2

The following section requires you to write a response to an expository prompt. You will have 30 minutes to complete this part of the test. A space has been provided for you to use for prewriting and organizing your thoughts. Remember, nothing on your prewrite page will be scored.

Use the lines provided to write your response to the prompt's questions. When you are finished writing, be sure to check over your work in this section only.

Once the 30 minutes is over, put your pencil down and close your book.

Writing Task

Each school year brings about new and interesting changes from the year before. Most students think of one school year as being their best.

Think about your years in school up until the present day. Which school year would you select as being the best one? Explain the things that made that school year so special.

GO ON

Prewriting and Planning

_____

_____

_____

_____

_____

_____

_____

_____

_____

_____

_____

_____

_____

_____

_____

GO ON

Your Response

Practice Test 1

Language Arts Literacy

Answers and Explanations

Day 1

Section 1

1. B

Asking questions in the beginning of a passage helps to engage and interest the reader about the topic.

2. C

Rigorous means strictly followed or demanding. The word **process** is a context clue to indicate there are many steps in becoming a marine biologist.

3. D

The author provides different examples of the sciences included under the topic of marine biology. The author would most likely agree that it is an extensive study of several different science practices.

4. C

Scientists use observations to conduct experiments that help them discover medicines and cures for disease and illness.

5. B

The article focuses on the many functions of marine biology. It explains how biologists study ocean and saltwater environments to help protect and preserve marine life.

6. A

Environmental biologists focus their studies on testing the health of the ocean so it is safe for all living creatures.

7. C

Since the Earth's surface is 70% water, scientists are constantly studying new environments; however, it makes it nearly impossible to discover unknown environments.

8. D

The article explains the work and discovery that biologists use to maintain a healthy environment. The article gives many ways that students, parents, and teachers can get actively involved in preserving marine life.

9. A

Studying oil spills allows scientists to study the long-term effects these spills have on marine life.

10. D

Only some of the studies of science that play an important role in the discoveries of marine biologists were mentioned in the article. Scientists from other fields would be expected to round out our perspective on marine life.

11. Open-Ended Question (Sample Response)

As the article explains, marine biologists help protect threatened species and habitats through research and observation. For example, through the observation and study of bacteria, scientists are able to understand the progression of the food chain. Scientists also study new organisms in hopes of creating medicine to cure disease and illness. I think it's extremely important to continue studying our marine life. Marine biologists hold the key to making new discoveries and uncovering valuable findings that help preserve and protect living creatures on our watery planet.

Day 1

Section 2

Writing Task (Sample Response)

A loud roar echoes in the deciduous forest and out crawls one of the largest feline land mammals in the world. If I could live the life of any animal for a day, I would experience life as a spotted jaguar.

"Chomp, chomp, chomp" is the sound a jaguar's powerful jaws make when they are stalking and hunting prey. Jaguars have an eclectic diet that consists of deer, eggs, frogs, and fish, and anything else that they can catch, which makes finding food almost effortless. Since their diet spreads over a wide range of plant and animal life, jaguars are also able to survive in many living spaces such as forests, swamps, mountains, and grasslands. They never have to worry about food or shelter!

"What's that up there in the trees?" Given that jaguars are able to climb, swim, and leap with ease, they are one of the most feared land mammals. The hardest part about taking on the life of a jaguar would be avoiding hunters and poachers. Being an endangered species means that a very small amount of jaguars are left in the world. Living a life where I am constantly running and hiding would be very lonely. Finding other jaguar friends would also be difficult if there were only a few others left in the world.

Trading places, trading spaces! If I could live the life of a jaguar for the day, I would jump at the chance to experience a day full of adventure. Being able to climb trees and watch other animals without the ability to be seen is very tempting; however, at the end of the day, I would be happier living a less dangerous life like my own. Besides, a jaguar can't ride his bike to the pool with his best friends on a hot summer day!

Day 1

Section 3

1. D

Kate Nease enjoys finding abstract moments and documenting them through her photos.

2. A

The article explains that most of Kate's photos are taken outdoors and that they capture nature. She uses nature as her background by photographing animals and people in a candid state.

3. D

Thinking quickly helps Kate document her subjects without interrupting their natural state. She enjoys unposed moments that require her to point and shoot without hesitation.

4. B

Digital technology is faster for shooting and uploading images. Kate Nease explains that her customers want instant gratification and expect to see the image right after it is taken.

5. C

The author makes it clear that Kate Nease's main goal is to capture moments for other people to remember forever.

6. C

By practicing unconventional methods, Kate is able to produce unique and personal photos without using props or posing her subjects.

7. A

Kate Nease enjoys the beauty of untouched nature; therefore, photographing the image of snow-covered tree branches would most likely interest her.

8. A

The word **vocation** means career. Kate Nease chose a career that travels with her.

9. B

The author's purpose was to describe one type of freelance photography. Through Kate Nease's experiences, the reader was able to connect to her way of taking photographs and understand the simplicity of nature.

10. D

Kate didn't interrupt the deer so that she could take a picture without scaring them. In doing so, Kate was able to capture a simple moment of a family of deer eating together.

11. Open-Ended Question (Sample Response)

"Kate Nease, a self-employed, freelance photographer, wants to accomplish one thing through her photos; to capture a memory." One ordinary moment that Kate Nease photographed happened while she was walking through the park on a spring day. She saw a mother deer and her babies grazing in the grass. Kate knew it was a simple yet extraordinary story she could tell through her camera. If I worked as a freelance photographer, I would take pictures that were both candid and posed. I think of weddings and birthday parties as joyous occasions that I would love to document. Everyone is always smiling and interacting with each other when they're having a good time. The pictures that I could take would remind people of how happy they were in that specific moment. Like Kate Nease, I also want my pictures to speak for themselves.

Day 2

Section 1

1. D

Juan and Lolita enjoyed going on adventures. The first paragraph indicates they had already explored many places such as the local parks, town pool, and school playground and were looking for a new and exciting activity.

2. C

A simile compares two things using **like** or **as**. In this case, the cabin was being compared to a shiny diamond because the walls were covered in mirrors and glass.

3. B

Paragraph 2 mentions that Cabin Cove was destroyed by a tornado.

4. A

By replacing the word **important** with **imperative**, the sentence remains true. **Minor** and **small** are both antonyms for the word **imperative**. **Exciting** is a good choice, but it is not the best replacement.

5. D

Juan and Lolita chose a potion that would benefit the greater good of their town. Although they thought about picking a potion that would grant them magical powers, they decided to do a good deed and give the residents back the campsite of Cabin Cove.

6. A

A potion that guarantees straight A grades was the only suggestion not mentioned in the passage.

7. B

Monty explained that Lolita and Juan could not witness his magic. When they heard the leaves rustling and wind blowing, they chose to follow Monty's rule and not look back.

8. C

In the second paragraph, the author explained that the town couldn't raise money to continue renovating Cabin Cove.

9. B

The author's purpose was to entertain the reader by creating an adventure that many would love to be a part of.

10. A

Monty appeared in the doorway of the ruby-red cabin after Juan and Lolita discovered the magic potions.

11. Open-Ended Question (Sample Response)

Juan and Lolita were looking for an adventure and discovered a cabin with magic potions. It's possible that there were many different ways to save Cabin Cove after seeing a room filled with potions. Juan and Lolita could have uncovered a potion that grew a money tree. They could then use that money to donate to the town council. In the beginning of the passage, the author described that the town was struggling to raise the funds needed to complete the renovation process of Cabin Cove.

Although Lolita first wanted to choose a potion that would give superpowers, she realized that helping others was more important. I think Lolita was most adventurous in this story because she acted fearlessly on the adventure. She also reassured Juan that they weren't going to be in any danger when walking into the cabin. If it weren't for Lolita's bravery, she and Juan might have never discovered Monty and the magic potions.

Day 2

Section 2

Writing Task (Sample Response)

"Grab your beach chairs and sunscreen, ladies and gentlemen. Today is the perfect day to head to the beach!" reported the weatherman on the morning news. Hannah and Lucy were finally on summer vacation. The first thing on their to-do list was a trip to the beach.

"Did you pack the SPF 30?" asked Lucy from the other room. Lucy was making sure she and Hannah had everything they'd need for a great day at the beach. The last thing that either of them wanted was to start off their summer vacation with sunburn! When the cooler was packed with sandwiches and bottled water, the girls were on their way. After a short 20-minute drive, they unpacked their belongings from the car and headed towards the main entrance. As they walked down to the beach, Lucy spotted a huge sign by the lifeguard stand. When they got close enough to read the posting, they realized they were facing a huge dilemma.

"Rough surf due to inclement weather. No swimming today," Hannah read from the sign that was propped up in the sand.

"Oh, come on! What inclement weather? It's a beautiful sunny day," Lucy said. At that moment, black clouds rolled in and the thunder roared. Hannah and Lucy snatched up their belongings and ran to the boardwalk for cover. They ran into the closest shop they could find and Hannah shut the door behind them. Looking out through the glass doors, Lucy and Hannah couldn't help but feel disappointed. "This is not how we were supposed to spend our first day of summer," Lucy groaned.

"It's not that bad, Lucy. Look behind you!" yelled Hannah. The girls had run in so quickly, they hadn't realized they were standing in the boardwalk's arcade center. Lucy's mood suddenly changed. She sprinted as fast as a cheetah to the help desk and was greeted by a friendly employee.

"Are the arcade games open?" Lucy asked.

"Absolutely. In fact, since you two are the only ones here, the games are on the house," he said with a welcoming gesture.

Lucy and Hannah raced towards the basketball hoops and ring toss where they each won a goldfish and stuffed penguin. From there, they moved to the Skee-ball booth and proceeded to win copious amounts of tickets to cash in at the arcade's treasure box.

"All of that winning really made me hungry!" Hannah remarked. After grabbing popcorn and pizza from the arcade's café, Hannah and Lucy realized that the storm had passed and the sun was brightly shining outside. They gathered up all their winnings and thanked the polite employee for allowing them to wait out the storm in the arcade. When they walked outside, they noticed the "rough surf" sign had been taken down. The girls dropped their things on the sand and scurried towards the ocean. Although it was just about time to head home, they couldn't pass up the opportunity to frolic in the ocean water.

"That wasn't such an awful start to summer," Lucy mentioned to Hannah.

"Not at all! In fact, I'd wait out a storm with you any day," giggled Hannah.

Practice Test 2

Language Arts Literacy

Answers and Explanations

Day 1

Section 1

1. D

The passage gives us no proof that the girls were loyal to one another. Since no one would dare sit at their table, this tells the reader that they actually might not be admired by others and that they believe they can do whatever they please.

2. B

Students need to use deductive reasoning to arrive at this answer; they could be tempted to choose A or D. It was mentioned that Fran sits alone every day at the same table, and if she were truly embarrassed by her looks and didn't want to call attention to herself, she might wear clothes that fit correctly. After what unfolds in the cafeteria, and what Fran says about being humiliated at the end, the best choice is that she wants to avoid getting teased.

3. A

By saying that Fran doesn't try to look or act normal, the girls are trying to justify why they have the right to make fun of Fran. They are placing the blame on her. The harassment and the assumption that Fran knows people are talking about her do not answer the question.

4. B

The author asks for the most likely reason. Sara was watching the abuse happen and knew it was wrong. She wanted it to stop. Everyone at her table was taking part in the teasing, as were the rest of the students, so the most likely reason for not speaking up is that she thought her friends would be angry with her or give her a difficult time.

5. B

"Deafening silence" is an oxymoron, as it contains two contradictory terms. **Silence** is a lack of noise while something **deafening** is extremely loud.

6. A

The author is making a comparison between Sara's legs and heavy weights as she drags herself up the stairs. Sara's friends already headed home, so D would not be a good choice. Answer B is taking the comment literally rather than figuratively. There was no indication that Sara was being forced to make an apology. Sara is not looking forward to what she feels she needs to do, so A is the correct choice.

7. C

Themes B and D would not fit this story. Students might think of the group of girls as representing the "evil" in this selection and Fran representing the "good," but this is actually an assumption, as we really do not know much about Fran except that she is being bullied. As evidenced in this story, words can be very powerful and damaging at times, so C is the correct choice.

8. C

Fran's words to Sara make it quite clear that she wants people to notice her and to treat her like a human being. There is no reason to believe she is trying to become friends with Sara, and although people may sometimes look into someone's eyes to see if they are being truthful, this does not seem to be Fran's motive in this case.

9. D

Sara seems very sincere in her apology. She even questions why she doesn't have the courage to look Fran in the face. After Fran leaves, Sara's eyes fills up with tears, obviously ashamed of her own actions. Sara would probably not tell her friends about the incident as she was afraid to speak up in the cafeteria. The best answer, knowing what we do about Sara, is D, that she will return and attempt to correct her wrongdoings.

10. B

The awkward feeling between the girls was an uncomfortable one. They are staring at one another, and no one is speaking. **Awkward** can mean stubborn, clumsy, or bulky, but none of these answers would fit in the context of the sentence.

11. **Open-Ended Question (Sample Response)**

The incident in the cafeteria is a form of bullying. Firstly, a student is sitting all alone in isolation with no one paying any attention to her. Students are ostracizing her in that they never tried to approach her and invite her to eat with them. These are indirect forms of bullying. The taunting and teasing were direct forms of harassment, and the students did this with every intention of hurting Fran's feelings. They have been judging Fran by her looks and her clothing alone, without ever getting to know her.

Once Sara felt that unpleasant feeling come over her, she realized that what was occurring was wrong. It is very difficult to stand up to a group of bullies, especially when they are your friends. Sara knew she should have stopped the teasing, but was worried about her own reputation. Sara might have started by talking to her twin sister or just one of her friends, asking them to just "cut it out and leave her alone." It would have been a start, and if she was able to get one student on her side, she might have had a chance of stopping the taunting. She also might have gone to get a teacher immediately before the incident escalated.

Day 1

Section 2

Writing Task (Sample Response)

Ten minutes felt like hours as Jon glanced at the clock in the classroom, waiting impatiently for the bell to ring. His soccer team had a scrimmage planned against the Cougars on Thursday, the number one team in the league. Their last meeting ended with the Cougars on top by a score of 3-2, the result of a shootout. In his heart, Jon knew his team had more talent and couldn't wait to show it on the field.

"….And for homework I want you to study…" Jon barely heard a word his teacher was saying as his mind was focused on his team's last practice before the scrimmage.

Just as the bell was about to ring, Principal Brown's scratchy voice could be heard over the intercom. "Ughhh…" thought Jon to himself. "Now we'll never get out of here!"

"May I have everyone's attention please? It has come to my attention over the past few weeks that there have been a number of incidents regarding basketball games during lunchtime. The younger students have been knocked over, hit by basketballs, and have been losing their own space on the playground. Your teachers and I have discussed this with you numerous times, but I have not seen significant improvement. Therefore, beginning Monday, the basketball hoops will be gone and the game will be banned at our school during lunchtime. I'm sure you all understand the reasons for this decision. Safety is my number one priority."

You could hear a pin drop in room 207 at that moment. Disbelief. Confusion. Shock. Then as if the lights just came on after a blackout, the students came alive and loud opinions filled the air.

"Are you kidding me?" asked one student. "What does he expect us to do out there?"

"This has to be a joke!" shouted another. "Basketball is a fifth and sixth grade lunchtime tradition! Our tournaments actually get me through the morning!"

Girls and boys alike were in disgust about the change that would be occurring the following week. They were thinking about their hour of release time turning into an hour of boredom. The younger students had their climber and playground equipment. The 3rd and 4th graders had their kickball diamond. High Point Elementary School had no soccer field, so there was nothing left except "Wall Ball," and Jon shivered at the thought of that five days a week. His thoughts about his soccer scrimmage were long gone as he contemplated the plight of him and his classmates.

The bell signaled the end of class, and the students walked out sullenly, looking for their other 5th and 6th grade friends to discuss the sudden end to their fun at lunchtime. They all gathered around the front of the school. "We just can't allow this to happen," Jon stated firmly. "We have to think of something to change Mr. Brown's mind."

"We have three days left!" Gina replied hopelessly. "What can we possibly do in three days?"

As a few parents approached their children to see what was going on, the crowd got larger and larger. Everyone seemed to understand the disappointment of the students, but they also knew that once Mr. Brown made up his mind, there was rarely any way to change it. It was Jon's mom who spoke first. "Years ago, when Jon's older brother was in school, I remember they had made a decision to shorten the lunch period." Other parents began nodding their heads. "The students started a petition. They had parents and members of the community sign their list, too. They had a good argument to back themselves up, and the new rule was dropped."

You could feel the excitement in the crowd as Jon's mother spoke. The classmates knew what they had to do. Groups were formed to cover certain areas of the neighborhood. Parents volunteered to be in charge of each group, but they made it clear that the boys and girls were responsible for this job, not the adults. Within two days, the fifth and sixth graders had over five hundred signatures! Everyone was convinced it would work. Everyone except Jon, that is.

"We can't just place this list of names on his desk," he explained one morning while waiting for the bell to ring. "We need to back up our request with some good arguments. Don't you remember what my mom said?"

It seemed as if the students' balloons just popped as their smiles turned to looks of concern. "So we did all this for nothing?" asked one of the boys in the group.

"Not necessarily," Jon responded. "Let's meet during lunch and brainstorm some reasons that will convince Mr. Brown to change his mind. I know we can do this, guys. I am NOT going to let them take down our hoops!"

When the bell rang at 11:30, the classmates inhaled their lunches, then headed for the playground. Gina wrote down all the ideas that students came up with, and the group then narrowed it down to three strong arguments. Basketball was a great form of exercise, everyone played together so it created a strong bond amongst the classmates, and it was a tradition that had been a part of High Point Elementary School for years. Students also decided that they needed to keep the younger children safe, so boundary lines would be drawn and they would agree to consequences if the rules were not followed. Gina used her 15 minutes of silent reading time to type up what the group came up with so they could present their arguments and petition to the principal after school.

"Mom! Mom!" Jon roared as he bolted through the door of his house at 3:45. "It worked! It really worked! Mr. Brown listened to our arguments and decided he might have made his decision too quickly. He believes that we are really going to make it work this time. The hoops are staying up!"

Jon's mom gave him a big hug. "It took a lot of effort, but you all cooperated and worked together. That's what made the difference. I'm proud of you," she said with a smile as she rubbed Jon's hair playfully. "Now get into your soccer uniform! You have a scrimmage at 5:00, remember?"

Jon was thrilled to get his mind off of basketball and back on soccer. With the way his luck was going, he knew there was no way his team would let the Cougars defeat them. After all, he convinced the toughest principal around to change his mind! "Anything is possible!" Jon thought convincingly to himself.

Day 1

Section 3

1. B

A and C are important details of the story, but the main idea is about the great threat that deforestation and losing rain forests pose to orangutans.

2. D

Pollution is not talked about in the passage. Deforestation is occurring because of both illegal logging and the growth of the palm-oil industry.

3. A

The author makes a point to mention the fact that there is a group that supports the growth of the palm-oil industry because it creates a large number of jobs in an economically poor nation.

4. A

The author defines the term **arboreal** by using the strategy of placing a definition directly after the word. The reader must then find the one animal that does not make its home in a tree, namely the lion.

5. B

Cookies and soap are items that are totally different from one another. This is a way to show the large variety of items made with palm oil. The quote is not persuasive in nature (choices C or D) nor is it placing blame, which answer A would suggest.

6. D

Students will need to use context clues for this answer. The first sentence in the section, "Still, economic growth comes at a price," suggests that the nation needs to make money but cannot destroy itself in the process. "Setting guidelines" is another clue to what the word means in this passage. Students may be tempted to choose answer A, but if palm-oil companies become illegal, the economy will suffer.

7. D

The orangutan is resourceful, as it finds clever ways to use whatever is available to it (e.g., the leaves). A, B, and C all show ways animals use what they have to get what they need done. Answer D is correct became it is simply a fact about elephants.

8. A

The author does not suggest prohibiting the use of palm oil. Galdikas wants the reader to become aware and knowledgeable about palm oil products by reading labels to see which items are made with this ingredient. Since she is sympathetic to the plight of orangutans, B would not be a sensible answer.

9. C

There are plausible reasons why students might select any answer except for D. The words **most likely** are key here. The article is very informative in nature, however, the subtitles alone ("Can the jungle and its animals be saved?"..."Save the Rain Forests!") suggest that the article is persuasive. Galdikas even gives advice as to what we can do to help the orangutans and their habitat.

10. A

Doolittle is trying to show the vast amount of forest land that is being destroyed. Images of deserts are usually of vast, barren places. She is trying to create a picture of that here. Although students might consider this an example of exaggeration, sympathy is not what she is trying to attain through her statement.

11. Open-Ended Question (Sample Response)

One reason that rain forests are at risk is because loggers are illegally chopping down the trees. By doing this, orangutans are losing their homes. In addition, the palm-oil industry creates many jobs in Indonesia, but at the risk of clearing large areas of forests. Deforestation "has claimed nearly 80% of the apes' jungle home."

Rain forests are important to both humans and animals. The trees in the forests give off oxygen, which humans need, and reduce the carbon dioxide which is harmful to our environment. Without these trees to absorb the CO_2, it stays in the air and may cause unhealthy changes to our climate.

Orangutans, among many other animals, are losing their homes. They are an endangered species. Once their habitats are destroyed, they have no way to survive.

Day 2

Section 1

1. A

"Go Fly a Kite" is a very common idiom which means "Go away...get out of here." The author uses this for a bit of humor, as the passage is informational in nature and not meant to be funny. Making a kite when you are bored and instructions for making one are small details only mentioned briefly in the story, so answers B and D would not be the reasons for the title.

2. C

The story of Han Hsin mentions an emperor, but does not explain his role, so B would not be the correct choice. Han Hsin uses the kite in a creative way to defeat the cruel emperor. The author is clearly giving the reader an example of a different way a kite was used in the past.

3. B

The passage stated that "at times, a kite could not get high enough to gather information" about temperature and wind speed. As explained in the story, the kites were tied together to help lift the first kite higher.

4. B

The words **most probable** are key here. Students might be tempted to choose answer A, thinking that smooth silk might make the string easier to hold, but it would actually make it more difficult as it would slip from a person's hands. C and D are unlikely choices, so the logical answer is B, even if the students do not know that silk is a poor conductor of electricity. Students may also use context clues, as the author talks about the dangers of using metal when making a kite and the author warns to stay away from power lines altogether.

5. D

Students need to focus on the word **contrast** in this question. The passage does not talk about the different looks of ancient and modern kites. Explaining the many different uses of kites over the years is not demonstrating one particular contrast. The main contrast is between the uses of ancient kites and those of modern ones.

6. C

The author of this story never leads the reader to believe he feels that one use of a kite is superior to another. He suggests making a kite on a rainy day, but there is no reason to think that he feels this is the best rainy day activity. Since the article is about the variety of uses of kites over the years, the best answer would be C.

7. A

There is not enough information in this passage for a student to learn how to make a kite, to learn about China's culture, or to write a report about Children's Day. Choice A is the best answer for this question.

8. D

Students need to determine the main idea of paragraph 13 in order to come up with a summary statement. Choices A and D are facts, but only details—not the main theme—about the paragraph. A point can be made that the reader may infer that boys are regarded highly in Japan, but this does not summarize the paragraph. Therefore, D is the correct answer.

9. C

The author states that Franklin was successful but also lucky. "Luck" in this context does not mean fame and fortune, as answers A and D would suggest. Franklin would not have conducted the experiment on a day that did not have the correct type of weather for it to work, so the correct answer is C. The author is referring to the dangers of the experiment.

10. B

Paragraph one has many examples of personification such as "A kite catches the wind," "The kite climbs higher and higher...," etc. It gives human traits to a non-human object. Similes and metaphors make comparisons, and there are none of these in paragraph one. There are no examples of extreme exaggeration, so answer A would not be correct.

11. Open-Ended Question (Sample Response)

One way kites were used in the past was for protection. Cameras were once tied to kites in order to take pictures from high up in the air. It was a way of keeping track of what enemy forces were doing. Kites were also used as targets during World War II to practice shooting. This was important because we didn't have the type of equipment we have now to keep our country safe.

Kites have also been used for cultural traditions in different countries. Kites' Day is a special day in China; it occurs on September 9 every year. Brightly colored kites are flown on this day by Chinese families in recognition of an old legend. The celebration is said to bring good luck to the Chinese people.

In Japan, there is another tradition called Children's Day. Boys and girls come out to fly their kites and put out their windsocks on May 5. The windsocks, which are shaped like strong fish called carp, are symbols of hard work and courage. The Japanese people believe these two traits are needed to be successful in life.

Culture and tradition are important. They are ways for families to celebrate their heritage and to enjoy fun times together.

Day 2

Section 2

Writing Task (Sample Response)

I consider myself to be very lucky in that I have enjoyed every grade in school so far. My teachers have all cared about me, kept me safe, and made learning special. I have wonderful memories of Kindergarten through Grade 5, and I will keep them with me always. If I had to pick one grade that stands out from all the others, I would have to choose Grade 4. There are so many reasons why my 4th grade year was so very special for me.

To begin with, I had the best teacher in the whole wide world! Mrs. K made an impression on me from the first day of school. She wanted to learn all about each one of us: our likes and dislikes, strengths and weaknesses, what we were expecting out of 4th grade—just everything! She made it into a game, so it helped us all learn about each other. I left school that day knowing it would be a good year.

My most difficult subject has always been math, but Mrs. K helped me whenever I needed it. She did it in a way that did not embarrass me or make me feel inferior to my classmates. In fact, she even taught me little games that I could use at home to help me understand new concepts better. I felt successful in her class, and that was so important to me.

There were so many special activities in Grade 4, too. For the first time, I was allowed to participate in our school's Track and Field Day! Before then, we were only allowed to go outside to watch. I was so excited to be a part of the long jump and the shuttle run. Even though I didn't win, I will never forget how it felt to be on the track with my family and classmates cheering me on! It was such a thrill for me!

Fourth graders learn all about our state of New Jersey, and boy did Mrs. K make it fun!! We researched our 21 counties, made a digital movie about what made each one special, learned a cool New Jersey song, and baked a cake in the shape of our state (with our parents' help, of course)! I will never forget our New Jersey Cake Day celebration! We ordered t-shirts with pictures of our parents' license plates on them and all wore them to put on a presentation for our parents. The best part was eating the cake! It was scrumptious!

My favorite part of the day in Fourth Grade was read-aloud time. Right after lunch, we had time to wind down by reading our own books quietly on the carpet or at our desks. After that, it was Mrs. K's turn to read to us. Her voice is hard to explain, but when she read, I felt as if I was right there in the book! I could picture people and places so vividly when she read to us. She could make me laugh out loud just by changing the tone of her voice, or cringe in my seat when she was reading a frightening mystery. I think my love of reading is directly related to Mrs. K's read-alouds! I want to read as well as she does someday.

School is great and I have always loved it since my first day of Kindergarten. Fourth grade, however, holds a special place in my heart. I have a feeling no other grade will ever top it!

Use this *page* to write your responses to the practice tests.

Use this *page* to write your responses to the practice tests.

Use this *page* to write your responses to the practice tests.

Use this page to write your responses to the practice tests.

Use this *page* to write your responses to the practice tests.

Use this page to write your responses to the practice tests.

Use this *page* to write your responses to the practice tests.

Use this *page* to write your responses to the practice tests.

Use this *page* to write your responses to the practice tests.

Use this *page* to write your responses to the practice tests.

Use this page to write your responses to the practice tests.